Ninja Foodi

Air Fryer

UK

Recipe Book

1001

Days Easy and Crispy Recipes for Beginners to Bake,
Air Fry, Grill and Roast in 2023

Kendrick D. McCartney

Warning-Disclaimer

The purpose of this book is to educate and entertain. The author or publisher does not guarantee that anyone following the techniques, suggestions, tips, ideas, or strategies will become successful. The author and publisher shall have neither liability or responsibility to anyone with respect to any loss or damage caused, or alleged to be caused, directly or indirectly by the information contained in this book.

Table of Contents

Chapter 6 Beef, Pork, and Lamb   35

Chapter 8 Vegetables and Sides   53

INTRODUCTION

We always want to cook healthy and the best meals for us and our loved ones at home. But due to our busy routines, we end up ordering food online every other day. So, we decided to help you make a switch to a healthier life with the Ninja Air Fryer cookbook.

So many people around the world just fell in love with the Ninja Air fryer and now it's your turn to join the crew. Our life has been completely changed since we bought this useful gadget and now we couldn't stop raving about having an air fryer in a modern kitchen. It will minimise time spent in the kitchen and make cooking less of a hassle and more fun. With Ninja, you'll be able to prepare multiple dishes like grilled meat, roasted veggies, pastries and your favourite fried foods all-in-one appliance, without conserving calories and saturated fat. The best part? You wouldn't have to worry about burnt skin from hot oil spillage. Remember how carefully you throw ingredients into the deep fryer to ensure that the hot oil doesn't spill and harm your skin?

Despite having an air fryer, there's one question that still bothers you: what to cook today? You probably run out of ideas or want to try something new and that's why we've created this recipe collection to help you get enough cooking inspo to fire up your kitchen game throughout the entire month. This cookbook contains super-easy, all-new recipes that make every day worthy of a celebration. Whether it's scrumptious, homestyle steak, grilled fish, roasted veggies, grilled appetisers, or mouthwatering dessert, you'll become an all-category cooking champion with this recipe cookbook.

It has recipes for weeknights when you don't want to think about dinner, crave-worthy breakfast recipes, traditional deep fried food recipes, lunch recipes, fish and seafood recipes, meat and poultry recipes. Whether you just unboxed your Ninja air fryer or are a beginner cook in general, this list of recipes is exactly what you need. They use simple ingredients, but pack a lot of flavour, and are super easy to make with step by step instructions that will make cooking a breeze even for amateur chefs. By making all types of healthier and tastier meal varieties, you'll be able to delight everyone in the family, even the picky eater. It'll be worth it when you see the smile on your loved ones' faces.

So without wasting your time, fire up your Ninja and let's Air Fry!

Chapter 1 The Basics! Embrace One-touch Cooking Experience at Home

Frying with minimal to no oil will make you think about the loss of flavour and texture but it's not the case with the Air fryer. Air fried food will still give that great crispiness and flavour you enjoy with traditional frying but with less fat and calories. It gives you a lighter option without sacrificing flavour and texture of food. We've found our air fryer excellent for jacket potatoes because we got perfectly baked spuds with crispy skins (same as oven baked). With its multiple cooking functions, family-sized capacity, and dishwasher safe parts, cooking will be more of a joyful experience. It will transform your favourite, comforting foods into healthy, low-cal dishes with tons of flavour and have everyone admire your cooking skills.

How Does the Ninja Air Fryer Work?

The Ninja Air Fryer circulates super-hot air around your food to crisp it up and remove moisture from its surface to give it that golden-brown finish with barely any oil needed. With rapid air technology, the Ninja air fryer cooks food in a way that's succulent on the inside and perfectly cooked on the outside. There's a heating element inside that distributes hot air around the food through a fan in circular motions to ensure quick cooking. The beauty of the Ninja air fryer is that you'll be using significantly less oil than traditional frying and you won't need paper kitchen towels to blot your food onto them.

With its multiple one-touch preset cooking temperatures that work for a variety of meals, even the new chefs can make delicious meals with minimal guidance regarding quantities of ingredients. If you want to achieve a more brownish, restaurant-style texture, don't overfill the basket. Leave the space between ingredients to allow the air to circulate effectively and reach all sides of the food. So far, the Ninja air fryer has earned 4.7 stars from nearly 15,000 customers on Amazon. They say it looks great on the counter, is easy to clean, and has fast cook times.

5 Awe-Inspiring Features for Versatile Cooking

Cooking in Ninja is simply a relaxed experience as it's packed with an array of features for hassle-free cooking. It allows you to prepare multiple recipes, not only the ones you'd traditionally sling in your deep fryer.

6 Cooking Functions

It's more than an air fryer with simple touchscreen controls. You can easily switch between Max Crisp, Roast, Bake, Reheat, Dehydrate and Air Fry functions. With its Air fry function, you can use little to no oil to create a deliciously crispy finish. While its Max crisp enables you to cook from frozen to crispy in minutes. Its Roast function allows you to get golden roast potatoes, balsamic tomatoes, and crispy crackling in minutes. You can also bake pasta, savoury pies, fresh bread, cakes, cookies and desserts with its bake function. And even cook frozen food with dehydrate function without defrosting. Its Reheat option helps restore leftovers to that fresh-out-of-the-oven finish.

Less Fat

Cooking in Ninja means 75% less fat in your food than you would have in your traditional fried foods. When compared to hand-cut, deep fried French Fries, it gives you the same great taste and crispness with little to no oil.

Faster Cooking

If you have a busy lifestyle and need to cook food in 15 to 25 minutes, Ninja is your saviour. It cooks food up to 50% faster than fan ovens without compromising the flavours. You can make one portion of frozen chips in 7-8 minutes with a crispy, golden texture or even bake a cake within 25 minutes, allowing you to manage your busy life.

Ideal Capacity

The Ninja air fryer has a family-sized 5.2L non-stick, removable basket to cook large portions of meals in one setting. This bulk capacity makes it ideal for big families, occasional treats, or cooking meals at the weekend and storing it in portions to eat the following week or as needed.

Cost Saving

People also praise the Ninja air fryer because it is highly economical and more energy-efficient than a conventional oven; thus saving you money on monthly energy bills.

Ninja Air Fryer Cooking Tips to Help You Become a Cooking Maestro

Having trouble deciding how to cook in your Ninja air fryer? How long does it cook? Do you need to flip the ingredients during cooking? Can I use oil? We've all been there - wondering how to make our favourite meals in this new kitchen gadget without burning. Here are some of our tried and tested cooking tips to help you use your air fryer correctly to achieve good results.

♦ Do a test run to remove the plastic/chemical smell before cooking.

♦ For thorough cooking, always preheat your Ninja Air Fryer before placing food inside for 3 to 5 minutes and ensure to use the crisper plate when you air fry for overall browning.

♦ If you are cooking chips, pull the pan out twice or thrice to give them a shake for no more than 30 seconds, and toss other food ingredients with silicone-tipped tongs to get them as crispy as you'd like.

◆ When you pull out the basket, the unit will automatically pause cooking and when you put it back, it will resume cooking.

◆ If you want to try different oven recipes in an air fryer, convert the recipe times by using the Roast or Bake function and reduce the temperature by 10°C.

◆ If you are cooking vegetables, use at least 15 mL of oil to achieve your desired level of crispiness. You can also use light cooking oil sprays to give a couple of squirts before cooking to crisp them up.

◆ Pat dry fruits and vegetables before placing them in the pan to dehydrate. The process of dehydration for most foods takes 6–8 hours while jerky takes 5–7 hours for a crispier result.

◆ Finish off dehydrated meats and fish by using the Roast function at 160°C for 1 minute to fully pasteurise them.

◆ Always secure lightweight ingredients with cocktail sticks and pour out fat drippings after cooking to avoid white smoke.

Care and Cleaning Tips to Keep Your Ninja Perfectly Shipshape

To ensure optimal performance of your air fryer and make it smell fresh, always clean it after every use so that no leftover food particles stick to places and create mess. If you leave the air fryer dirty with leftover food particles, it results in slower heating and more energy consumption.

Follow these tips to clean up your air fryer and make it look fresh:

◆ The basket is easy to clean by hand because of the non-stick coating and you can also put it in a dishwasher (but it's rather bulky for it).

◆ To handwash your basket and other removable accessories, soak them in hot soapy water for about 10 minutes and use a non-abrasive sponge to clean all the food debris.

◆ For stubborn grease, mix 30 mL baking soda and 15 mL water to form a paste and apply it using a sponge. Scrub and leave them for 15 minutes and then rinse.

◆ Clean the unit inside out with a damp cloth and make sure you do not scrub the interior heating element. It may damage the heating mechanism.

◆ Once you clean all the removable parts and dry clean them and reassemble the unit for the next use.

Chapter 2 Breakfasts

Bacon, Egg, and Cheese Roll Ups

Prep time: 15 minutes | Cook time: 15 minutes | Serves 4

2 tablespoons unsalted butter
60 ml chopped onion
½ medium green pepper, seeded and chopped
6 large eggs
12 slices bacon
235 ml shredded sharp Cheddar cheese
120 ml mild salsa, for dipping

1. In a medium skillet over medium heat, melt butter. Add onion and pepper to the skillet and sauté until fragrant and onions are translucent, about 3 minutes. 2. Whisk eggs in a small bowl and pour into skillet. Scramble eggs with onions and peppers until fluffy and fully cooked, about 5 minutes. Remove from heat and set aside. 3. On work surface, place three slices of bacon side by side, overlapping about ¼ inch. Place 60 ml scrambled eggs in a heap on the side closest to you and sprinkle 60 ml cheese on top of the eggs. 4. Tightly roll the bacon around the eggs and secure the seam with a toothpick if necessary. Place each roll into the air fryer basket. 5. Adjust the temperature to 176ºC and air fry for 15 minutes. Rotate the rolls halfway through the cooking time. 6. Bacon will be brown and crispy when completely cooked. Serve immediately with salsa for dipping.

Kale and Potato Nuggets

Prep time: 10 minutes | Cook time: 18 minutes | Serves 4

1 teaspoon extra virgin olive oil
1 clove garlic, minced
1 L kale, rinsed and chopped
475 ml potatoes, boiled and mashed
30 ml milk
Salt and ground black pepper, to taste
Cooking spray

1. Preheat the air fryer to 200ºC. 2. In a skillet over medium heat, sauté the garlic in the olive oil, until it turns golden brown. Sauté with the kale for an additional 3 minutes and remove from the heat. 3. Mix the mashed potatoes, kale and garlic in a bowl. Pour in the milk and sprinkle with salt and pepper. 4. Shape the mixture into nuggets and spritz with cooking spray. 5. Put in the air fryer basket and air fry for 15 minutes, flip the nuggets halfway through cooking to make sure the nuggets fry evenly. 6. Serve immediately.

Chimichanga Breakfast Burrito

Prep time: 10 minutes | Cook time: 10 minutes | Serves 2

2 large (10- to 12-inch) flour tortillas
120 ml canned refried beans (pinto or black work equally well)
4 large eggs, cooked scrambled
4 corn tortilla chips, crushed
120 ml grated chili cheese
12 pickled jalapeño slices
1 tablespoon vegetable oil
Guacamole, salsa, and sour cream, for serving (optional)

1. Place the tortillas on a work surface and divide the refried beans between them, spreading them in a rough rectangle in the center of the tortillas. Top the beans with the scrambled eggs, crushed chips, cheese, and jalapeños. Fold one side over the fillings, then fold in each short side and roll up the rest of the way like a burrito. 2. Brush the outside of the burritos with the oil, then transfer to the air fryer, seam-side down. Air fry at 176ºC until the tortillas are browned and crisp and the filling is warm throughout, about 10 minutes. 3. Transfer the chimichangas to plates and serve warm with guacamole, salsa, and sour cream, if you like.

Peppered Maple Bacon Knots

Prep time: 5 minutes | Cook time: 7 to 8 minutes | Serves 6

450 g maple smoked/cured bacon rashers
60 ml maple syrup
60 ml brown sugar
Coarsely cracked black peppercorns, to taste

1. Preheat the air fryer to 200ºC. 2. On a clean work surface, tie each bacon strip in a loose knot. 3. Stir together the maple syrup and brown sugar in a bowl. Generously brush this mixture over the bacon knots. 4. Working in batches, arrange the bacon knots in the air fryer basket. Sprinkle with the coarsely cracked black peppercorns. 5. Air fry for 5 minutes. Flip the bacon knots and continue cooking for 2 to 3 minutes more, or until the bacon is crisp. 6. Remove from the basket to a paper towel-lined plate. Repeat with the remaining bacon knots. 7. Let the bacon knots cool for a few minutes and serve warm.

Lemon-Blueberry Muffins

Prep time: 5 minutes | Cook time: 20 to 25 minutes | Makes 6

muffins

300 ml almond flour	3 tablespoons melted butter
3 tablespoons granulated sweetener	1 tablespoon almond milk
	1 tablespoon fresh lemon juice
1 teaspoon baking powder	120 ml fresh blueberries
2 large eggs	

1. Preheat the air fryer to 176ºC. Lightly coat 6 silicone muffin cups with vegetable oil. Set aside. 2. In a large mixing bowl, combine the almond flour, sweetener, and baking soda. Set aside. 3. In a separate small bowl, whisk together the eggs, butter, milk, and lemon juice. Add the egg mixture to the flour mixture and stir until just combined. Fold in the blueberries and let the batter sit for 5 minutes. 4. Spoon the muffin batter into the muffin cups, about two-thirds full. Air fry for 20 to 25 minutes, or until a toothpick inserted into the center of a muffin comes out clean. 5. Remove the basket from the air fryer and let the muffins cool for about 5 minutes before transferring them to a wire rack to cool completely.

Bacon Eggs on the Go

Prep time: 5 minutes | Cook time: 15 minutes | Serves 1

2 eggs	Salt and ground black pepper,
110 g bacon, cooked	to taste

1. Preheat the air fryer to 204ºC. Put liners in a regular cupcake tin. 2. Crack an egg into each of the cups and add the bacon. Season with some pepper and salt. 3. Bake in the preheated air fryer for 15 minutes, or until the eggs are set. Serve warm.

Sausage Egg Cup

Prep time: 10 minutes | Cook time: 15 minutes | Serves 6

340 g pork sausage, removed from casings	¼ teaspoon ground black pepper
6 large eggs	½ teaspoon crushed red pepper
½ teaspoon salt	flakes

1. Place sausage in six 4-inch ramekins (about 60 g per ramekin) greased with cooking oil. Press sausage down to cover bottom and about ½-inch up the sides of ramekins. Crack one egg into each ramekin and sprinkle evenly with salt, black pepper, and red pepper flakes. 2. Place ramekins into air fryer basket. Adjust the temperature to 176ºC and set the timer for 15 minutes. Egg cups will be done when sausage is fully cooked to at least 64ºC and the egg is firm. Serve warm.

Berry Muffins

Prep time: 15 minutes | Cook time: 12 to 17 minutes | Makes 8

muffins

315 ml plus 1 tablespoon plain flour, divided	2 eggs
	160 ml whole milk
60 ml granulated sugar	80 ml neutral oil
2 tablespoons light brown sugar	235 ml mixed fresh berries
2 teaspoons baking powder	

1. In a medium bowl, stir together 315 ml of flour, the granulated sugar, brown sugar, and baking powder until mixed well. 2. In a small bowl, whisk the eggs, milk, and oil until combined. Stir the egg mixture into the dry ingredients just until combined. 3. In another small bowl, toss the mixed berries with the remaining 1 tablespoon of flour until coated. Gently stir the berries into the batter. 4. Double up 16 foil muffin cups to make 8 cups. 5. Insert the crisper plate into the basket and the basket into the unit. Preheat the unit by selecting BAKE, setting the temperature to 156ºC, and setting the time to 3 minutes. Select START/STOP to begin. 6. Once the unit is preheated, place 1 L into the basket and fill each three-quarters full with the batter. 7. Select BAKE, set the temperature to 156ºC, and set the time for 17 minutes. Select START/STOP to begin. 8. After about 12 minutes, check the muffins. If they spring back when lightly touched with your finger, they are done. If not, resume cooking. 9. When the cooking is done, transfer the muffins to a wire rack to cool. 10. Repeat steps 6, 7, and 8 with the remaining muffin cups and batter. 11. Let the muffins cool for 10 minutes before serving.

Italian Egg Cups

Prep time: 5 minutes | Cook time: 10 minutes | Serves 4

Olive oil	4 teaspoons grated Parmesan
235 ml marinara sauce	cheese
4 eggs	Salt and freshly ground black
4 tablespoons shredded	pepper, to taste
Mozzarella cheese	Chopped fresh basil, for garnish

1. Lightly spray 4 individual ramekins with olive oil. 2. Pour 60 ml marinara sauce into each ramekin. 3. Crack one egg into each ramekin on top of the marinara sauce. 4. Sprinkle 1 tablespoon of Mozzarella and 1 tablespoon of Parmesan on top of each egg. Season with salt and pepper. 5. Cover each ramekin with aluminum foil. Place two of the ramekins in the air fryer basket. 6. Air fry at 176ºC for 5 minutes and remove the aluminum foil. Air fry until the top is lightly browned and the egg white is cooked, another 2 to 4 minutes. If you prefer the yolk to be firmer, cook for 3 to 5 more minutes. 7. Repeat with the remaining two ramekins. Garnish with basil and serve.

Spinach Omelet

Prep time: 5 minutes | Cook time: 12 minutes | Serves 2

4 large eggs	2 tablespoons salted butter, melted
350 ml chopped fresh spinach leaves	
2 tablespoons peeled and chopped brown onion	120 ml shredded mild Cheddar cheese
	¼ teaspoon salt

1. In an ungreased round nonstick baking dish, whisk eggs. Stir in spinach, onion, butter, Cheddar, and salt. 2. Place dish into air fryer basket. Adjust the temperature to 160ºC and bake for 12 minutes. Omelet will be done when browned on the top and firm in the middle. 3. Slice in half and serve warm on two medium plates.

Spinach and Mushroom Mini Quiche

Prep time: 10 minutes | Cook time: 15 minutes | Serves 4

1 teaspoon olive oil, plus more for spraying	120 ml shredded Cheddar cheese
235 ml coarsely chopped mushrooms	120 ml shredded Mozzarella cheese
235 ml fresh baby spinach, shredded	¼ teaspoon salt
	¼ teaspoon black pepper
4 eggs, beaten	

1. Spray 4 silicone baking cups with olive oil and set aside. 2. In a medium sauté pan over medium heat, warm 1 teaspoon of olive oil. Add the mushrooms and sauté until soft, 3 to 4 minutes. 3. Add the spinach and cook until wilted, 1 to 2 minutes. Set aside. 4. In a medium bowl, whisk together the eggs, Cheddar cheese, Mozzarella cheese, salt, and pepper. 5. Gently fold the mushrooms and spinach into the egg mixture. 6. Pour ¼ of the mixture into each silicone baking cup. 7. Place the baking cups into the air fryer basket and air fry at 176ºC for 5 minutes. Stir the mixture in each ramekin slightly and air fry until the egg has set, an additional 3 to 5 minutes.

Buffalo Chicken Breakfast Muffins

Prep time: 7 minutes | Cook time: 13 to 16 minutes | Serves 10

170 g shredded cooked chicken	1 teaspoon minced garlic
85 g blue cheese, crumbled	6 large eggs
2 tablespoons unsalted butter, melted	Sea salt and freshly ground black pepper, to taste
80 ml Buffalo hot sauce, such as Frank's RedHot	Avocado oil spray

1. In a large bowl, stir together the chicken, blue cheese, melted butter, hot sauce, and garlic. 2. In a medium bowl or large liquid measuring cup, beat the eggs. Season with salt and pepper. 3. Spray 10 silicone muffin cups with oil. Divide the chicken mixture among the cups, and pour the egg mixture over top. 4. Place the cups in the air fryer and set to 150ºC. Bake for 13 to 16 minutes, until the muffins are set and cooked through. (Depending on the size of your air fryer, you may need to cook the muffins in batches.)

Cheddar Eggs

Prep time: 5 minutes | Cook time: 15 minutes | Serves 2

4 large eggs	120 ml shredded sharp Cheddar cheese
2 tablespoons unsalted butter, melted	

1. Crack eggs into a round baking dish and whisk. Place dish into the air fryer basket. 2. Adjust the temperature to 204ºC and set the timer for 10 minutes. 3. After 5 minutes, stir the eggs and add the butter and cheese. Let cook 3 more minutes and stir again. 4. Allow eggs to finish cooking an additional 2 minutes or remove if they are to your desired liking. 5. Use a fork to fluff. Serve warm.

Apple Rolls

Prep time: 20 minutes | Cook time: 20 to 24 minutes | Makes 12 rolls

Apple Rolls:	sugar
475 ml plain flour, plus more for dusting	1 teaspoon ground cinnamon
2 tablespoons granulated sugar	1 large Granny Smith apple, peeled and diced
1 teaspoon salt	1 to 2 tablespoons oil
3 tablespoons butter, at room temperature	Icing:
180 ml milk, whole or semi-skimmed	120 ml icing sugar
	½ teaspoon vanilla extract
120 ml packed light brown	2 to 3 tablespoons milk, whole or semi-skimmed

Make the Apple Rolls 1. In a large bowl, whisk the flour, granulated sugar, and salt until blended. Stir in the butter and milk briefly until a sticky dough forms. 2. In a small bowl, stir together the brown sugar, cinnamon, and apple. 3. Place a piece of parchment paper on a work surface and dust it with flour. Roll the dough on the prepared surface to ¼ inch thickness. 4. Spread the apple mixture over the dough. Roll up the dough jelly roll-style, pinching the ends to seal. Cut the dough into 12 rolls. 5. Preheat the air fryer to 160ºC. 6. Line the air fryer basket with parchment paper and spritz it with oil. Place 6 rolls on the prepared parchment. 7. Bake for 5 minutes. Flip the rolls and bake for 5 to 7 minutes more until lightly browned. Repeat with the remaining rolls. Make the Icing 8. In a medium bowl, whisk the icing sugar, vanilla, and milk until blended. 9. Drizzle over the warm rolls.

Tomato and Mozzarella Bruschetta

Prep time: 5 minutes | Cook time: 4 minutes | Serves 1

6 small loaf slices
120 ml tomatoes, finely chopped
85 g Mozzarella cheese, grated

1 tablespoon fresh basil, chopped
1 tablespoon olive oil

1. Preheat the air fryer to 176°C. 2. Put the loaf slices inside the air fryer and air fry for about 3 minutes. 3. Add the tomato, Mozzarella, basil, and olive oil on top. 4. Air fry for an additional minute before serving.

Keto Quiche

Prep time: 10 minutes | Cook time: 1 hour | Makes 1 (6-inch) quiche

Crust:
300 ml blanched almond flour
300 ml grated Parmesan or Gouda cheese
¼ teaspoon fine sea salt
1 large egg, beaten
Filling:
120 ml chicken or beef stock (or vegetable stock for vegetarian)
235 ml shredded Swiss cheese (about 110 g)

110 g cream cheese (120 ml)
1 tablespoon unsalted butter, melted
4 large eggs, beaten
80 ml minced leeks or sliced spring onions
¾ teaspoon fine sea salt
⅛ teaspoon cayenne pepper
Chopped spring onions, for garnish

1. Preheat the air fryer to 164°C. Grease a pie pan. Spray two large pieces of parchment paper with avocado oil and set them on the countertop. 2. Make the crust: In a medium-sized bowl, combine the flour, cheese, and salt and mix well. Add the egg and mix until the dough is well combined and stiff. 3. Place the dough in the center of one of the greased pieces of parchment. Top with the other piece of parchment. Using a rolling pin, roll out the dough into a circle about 1/16 inch thick. 4. Press the pie crust into the prepared pie pan. Place it in the air fryer and bake for 12 minutes, or until it starts to lightly brown. 5. While the crust bakes, make the filling: In a large bowl, combine the stock, Swiss cheese, cream cheese, and butter. Stir in the eggs, leeks, salt, and cayenne pepper. When the crust is ready, pour the mixture into the crust. 6. Place the quiche in the air fryer and bake for 15 minutes. Turn the heat down to 150°C and bake for an additional 30 minutes, or until a knife inserted 1 inch from the edge comes out clean. You may have to cover the edges of the crust with foil to prevent burning. 7. Allow the quiche to cool for 10 minutes before garnishing it with chopped spring onions and cutting it into wedges. 8. Store leftovers in an airtight container in the refrigerator for up to 4 days or in the freezer for up to a month. Reheat in a preheated 176°C air fryer for a few minutes, until warmed through.

Pizza Eggs

Prep time: 5 minutes | Cook time: 10 minutes | Serves 2

235 ml shredded Mozzarella cheese
7 slices pepperoni, chopped
1 large egg, whisked

¼ teaspoon dried oregano
¼ teaspoon dried parsley
¼ teaspoon garlic powder
¼ teaspoon salt

1. Place Mozzarella in a single layer on the bottom of an ungreased round nonstick baking dish. Scatter pepperoni over cheese, then pour egg evenly around baking dish. 2. Sprinkle with remaining ingredients and place into air fryer basket. Adjust the temperature to 166°C and bake for 10 minutes. When cheese is brown and egg is set, dish will be done. 3. Let cool in dish 5 minutes before serving.

Super Easy Bacon Cups

Prep time: 5 minutes | Cook time: 20 minutes | Serves 2

3 slices bacon, cooked, sliced in half
2 slices ham
1 slice tomato
2 eggs

2 teaspoons grated Parmesan cheese
Salt and ground black pepper, to taste

1. Preheat the air fryer to 192°C. Line 2 greased muffin tins with 3 half-strips of bacon 2. Put one slice of ham and half slice of tomato in each muffin tin on top of the bacon 3. Crack one egg on top of the tomato in each muffin tin and sprinkle each with half a teaspoon of grated Parmesan cheese. Sprinkle with salt and ground black pepper, if desired. 4. Bake in the preheated air fryer for 20 minutes. Remove from the air fryer and let cool. 5. Serve warm.

Cajun Breakfast Sausage

Prep time: 10 minutes | Cook time: 15 to 20 minutes | Serves 8

680 g 85% lean turkey mince
3 cloves garlic, finely chopped
¼ onion, grated
1 teaspoon Tabasco sauce

1 teaspoon Cajun seasoning
1 teaspoon dried thyme
½ teaspoon paprika
½ teaspoon cayenne

1. Preheat the air fryer to 188°C. 2. In a large bowl, combine the turkey, garlic, onion, Tabasco, Cajun seasoning, thyme, paprika, and cayenne. Mix with clean hands until thoroughly combined. Shape into 16 patties, about ½ inch thick. (Wet your hands slightly if you find the sausage too sticky to handle.) 3. Working in batches if necessary, arrange the patties in a single layer in the air fryer basket. Pausing halfway through the cooking time to flip the patties, air fry for 15 to 20 minutes until a thermometer inserted into the thickest portion registers 74°C.

Pancake for Two

Prep time: 5 minutes | Cook time: 30 minutes | Serves 2

235 ml blanched finely ground almond flour

2 tablespoons granular erythritol

1 tablespoon salted butter,

melted

1 large egg

80 ml unsweetened almond milk

½ teaspoon vanilla extract

1. In a large bowl, mix all ingredients together, then pour half the batter into an ungreased round nonstick baking dish. 2. Place dish into air fryer basket. Adjust the temperature to 160ºC and bake for 15 minutes. The pancake will be golden brown on top and firm, and a toothpick inserted in the center will come out clean when done. Repeat with remaining batter. 3. Slice in half in dish and serve warm.

Bacon, Cheese, and Avocado Melt

Prep time: 5 minutes | Cook time: 3 to 5 minutes | Serves 2

1 avocado

4 slices cooked bacon, chopped

2 tablespoons salsa

1 tablespoon double cream

60 ml shredded Cheddar cheese

1. Preheat the air fryer to 204ºC. 2. Slice the avocado in half lengthwise and remove the stone. To ensure the avocado halves do not roll in the basket, slice a thin piece of skin off the base. 3. In a small bowl, combine the bacon, salsa, and cream. Divide the mixture between the avocado halves and top with the cheese. 4. Place the avocado halves in the air fryer basket and air fry for 3 to 5 minutes until the cheese has melted and begins to brown. Serve warm.

Southwestern Ham Egg Cups

Prep time: 5 minutes | Cook time: 12 minutes | Serves 2

4 (30 g) slices wafer-thin ham

4 large eggs

2 tablespoons full-fat sour cream

60 ml diced green pepper

2 tablespoons diced red pepper

2 tablespoons diced brown onion

120 ml shredded medium Cheddar cheese

1. Place one slice of ham on the bottom of four baking cups. 2. In a large bowl, whisk eggs with sour cream. Stir in green pepper, red pepper, and onion. 3. Pour the egg mixture into ham-lined baking cups. Top with Cheddar. Place cups into the air fryer basket. 4. Adjust the temperature to 160ºC and bake for 12 minutes or until the tops are browned. 5. Serve warm.

Egg Tarts

Prep time: 10 minutes | Cook time: 17 to 20 minutes | Makes 2 tarts

⅓ sheet frozen puff pastry, thawed

Cooking oil spray

120 ml shredded Cheddar cheese

2 eggs

¼ teaspoon salt, divided

1 teaspoon minced fresh parsley (optional)

1. Insert the crisper plate into the basket and the basket into the unit. Preheat the unit by selecting BAKE, setting the temperature to 200ºC, and setting the time to 3 minutes. Select START/STOP to begin. 2. Lay the puff pastry sheet on a piece of parchment paper and cut it in half. 3. Once the unit is preheated, spray the crisper plate with cooking oil. Transfer the 2 squares of pastry to the basket, keeping them on the parchment paper. 4. Select BAKE, set the temperature to 200ºC, and set the time to 20 minutes. Select START/STOP to begin. 5. After 10 minutes, use a metal spoon to press down the center of each pastry square to make a well. Divide the cheese equally between the baked pastries. Carefully crack an egg on top of the cheese, and sprinkle each with the salt. Resume cooking for 7 to 10 minutes. 6. When the cooking is complete, the eggs will be cooked through. Sprinkle each with parsley (if using) and serve.

Banana-Nut Muffins

Prep time: 5 minutes | Cook time: 15 minutes | Makes 10 muffins

Oil, for spraying

2 very ripe bananas

120 ml packed light brown sugar

80 ml rapeseed oil or vegetable oil

1 large egg

1 teaspoon vanilla extract

180 ml plain flour

1 teaspoon baking powder

1 teaspoon ground cinnamon

120 ml chopped walnuts

1. Preheat the air fryer to 160ºC. Spray 10 silicone muffin cups lightly with oil. 2. In a medium bowl, mash the bananas. Add the brown sugar, rapeseed oil, egg, and vanilla and stir to combine. 3. Fold in the flour, baking powder, and cinnamon until just combined. 4. Add the walnuts and fold a few times to distribute throughout the batter. 5. Divide the batter equally among the prepared muffin cups and place them in the basket. You may need to work in batches, depending on the size of your air fryer. 6. Cook for 15 minutes, or until golden brown and a toothpick inserted into the center of a muffin comes out clean. The air fryer tends to brown muffins more than the oven, so don't be alarmed if they are darker than you're used to. They will still taste great. 7. Let cool on a wire rack before serving.

Nutty Granola

Prep time: 5 minutes | Cook time: 1 hour | Serves 4

120 ml pecans, coarsely chopped	2 tablespoons sunflower seeds
120 ml walnuts or almonds, coarsely chopped	2 tablespoons melted butter
60 ml desiccated coconut	60 ml granulated sweetener
60 ml almond flour	½ teaspoon ground cinnamon
60 ml ground flaxseed or chia seeds	½ teaspoon vanilla extract
	¼ teaspoon ground nutmeg
	¼ teaspoon salt
	2 tablespoons water

1. Preheat the air fryer to 120°C. Cut a piece of parchment paper to fit inside the air fryer basket. 2. In a large bowl, toss the nuts, coconut, almond flour, ground flaxseed or chia seeds, sunflower seeds, butter, sweetener, cinnamon, vanilla, nutmeg, salt, and water until thoroughly combined. 3. Spread the granola on the parchment paper and flatten to an even thickness. 4. Air fry for about an hour, or until golden throughout. Remove from the air fryer and allow to fully cool. Break the granola into bite-size pieces and store in a covered container for up to a week.

Tomato and Cheddar Rolls

Prep time: 30 minutes | Cook time: 25 minutes | Makes 12 rolls

4 plum tomatoes	2 teaspoons sugar
½ clove garlic, minced	2 teaspoons salt
1 tablespoon olive oil	1 tablespoon olive oil
¼ teaspoon dried thyme	235 ml grated Cheddar cheese,
Salt and freshly ground black pepper, to taste	plus more for sprinkling at the end
1 L plain flour	350 ml water
1 teaspoon active dry yeast	

1. Cut the tomatoes in half, remove the seeds with your fingers and transfer to a bowl. Add the garlic, olive oil, dried thyme, salt and freshly ground black pepper and toss well. 2. Preheat the air fryer to 200°C. 3. Place the tomatoes, cut side up in the air fryer basket and air fry for 10 minutes. The tomatoes should just start to brown. Shake the basket to redistribute the tomatoes, and air fry for another 5 to 10 minutes at 166°C until the tomatoes are no longer juicy. Let the tomatoes cool and then rough chop them. 4. Combine the flour, yeast, sugar and salt in the bowl of a stand mixer. Add the olive oil, chopped roasted tomatoes and Cheddar cheese to the flour mixture and start to mix using the dough hook attachment. As you're mixing, add 300 ml of the water, mixing until the dough comes together. Continue to knead the dough with the dough hook for another 10 minutes, adding enough water to the dough to get it to the right consistency. 5. Transfer the dough to an oiled bowl, cover with a clean kitchen towel and let it rest and rise until it has

doubled in volume, about 1 to 2 hours. Then, divide the dough into 12 equal portions. Roll each portion of dough into a ball. Lightly coat each dough ball with oil and let the dough balls rest and rise a second time, covered lightly with plastic wrap for 45 minutes. (Alternately, you can place the rolls in the refrigerator overnight and take them out 2 hours before you bake them.) 6. Preheat the air fryer to 182°C. 7. Spray the dough balls and the air fryer basket with a little olive oil. Place three rolls at a time in the basket and bake for 10 minutes. Add a little grated Cheddar cheese on top of the rolls for the last 2 minutes of air frying for an attractive finish.

Hearty Cheddar Biscuits

Prep time: 10 minutes | Cook time: 22 minutes | Makes 8 biscuits

550 ml self-raising flour	plus more to melt on top
2 tablespoons sugar	315 ml buttermilk
120 ml butter, frozen for 15 minutes	235 ml plain flour, for shaping
120 ml grated Cheddar cheese,	1 tablespoon butter, melted

1. Line a buttered 7-inch metal cake pan with parchment paper or a silicone liner. 2. Combine the flour and sugar in a large mixing bowl. Grate the butter into the flour. Add the grated cheese and stir to coat the cheese and butter with flour. Then add the buttermilk and stir just until you can no longer see streaks of flour. The dough should be quite wet. 3. Spread the plain (not self-raising) flour out on a small cookie sheet. With a spoon, scoop 8 evenly sized balls of dough into the flour, making sure they don't touch each other. With floured hands, coat each dough ball with flour and toss them gently from hand to hand to shake off any excess flour. Put each floured dough ball into the prepared pan, right up next to the other. This will help the biscuits rise, rather than spreading out. 4. Preheat the air fryer to 192°C. 5. Transfer the cake pan to the basket of the air fryer. Let the ends of the aluminum foil sling hang across the cake pan before returning the basket to the air fryer. 6. Air fry for 20 minutes. Check the biscuits twice to make sure they are not getting too brown on top. If they are, re-arrange the aluminum foil strips to cover any brown parts. After 20 minutes, check the biscuits by inserting a toothpick into the center of the biscuits. It should come out clean. If it needs a little more time, continue to air fry for two extra minutes. Brush the tops of the biscuits with some melted butter and sprinkle a little more grated cheese on top if desired. Pop the basket back into the air fryer for another 2 minutes. 7. Remove the cake pan from the air fryer. Let the biscuits cool for just a minute or two and then turn them out onto a plate and pull apart. Serve immediately.

Spinach and Bacon Roll-ups

Prep time: 5 minutes | Cook time: 8 to 9 minutes | Serves 4

4 flour tortillas (6- or 7-inch size)
4 slices Swiss cheese
235 ml baby spinach leaves

4 slices turkey bacon
Special Equipment:
4 toothpicks, soak in water for at least 30 minutes

1. Preheat the air fryer to 200°C. 2. On a clean work surface, top each tortilla with one slice of cheese and 60 ml spinach, then tightly roll them up. 3. Wrap each tortilla with a strip of turkey bacon and secure with a toothpick. 4. Arrange the roll-ups in the air fryer basket, leaving space between each roll-up. 5. Air fry for 4 minutes. Flip the roll-ups with tongs and rearrange them for more even cooking. Air fry for another 4 to 5 minutes until the bacon is crisp. 6. Rest for 5 minutes and remove the toothpicks before serving.

Green Eggs and Ham

Prep time: 5 minutes | Cook time: 10 minutes | Serves 2

1 large Hass avocado, halved and pitted
2 thin slices ham
2 large eggs
2 tablespoons chopped spring onions, plus more for garnish

½ teaspoon fine sea salt
¼ teaspoon ground black pepper
60 ml shredded Cheddar cheese (omit for dairy-free)

1. Preheat the air fryer to 204°C. 2. Place a slice of ham into the cavity of each avocado half. Crack an egg on top of the ham, then sprinkle on the green onions, salt, and pepper. 3. Place the avocado halves in the air fryer cut side up and air fry for 10 minutes, or until the egg is cooked to your desired doneness. Top with the cheese (if using) and air fry for 30 seconds more, or until the cheese is melted. Garnish with chopped green onions. 4. Best served fresh. Store extras in an airtight container in the fridge for up to 4 days. Reheat in a preheated 176°C air fryer for a few minutes, until warmed through.

Easy Buttermilk Biscuits

Prep time: 5 minutes | Cook time: 18 minutes | Makes 16 biscuits

600 ml plain flour
1 tablespoon baking powder
1 teaspoon coarse or flaky salt
1 teaspoon sugar

½ teaspoon baking soda
8 tablespoons (1 stick) unsalted butter, at room temperature
235 ml buttermilk, chilled

1. Stir together the flour, baking powder, salt, sugar, and baking powder in a large bowl. 2. Add the butter and stir to mix well. Pour in the buttermilk and stir with a rubber spatula just until incorporated. 3. Place the dough onto a lightly floured surface and roll the dough out to a disk, ½ inch thick. Cut out the biscuits with a 2-inch round cutter and re-roll any scraps until you have 16 biscuits. 4. Preheat the air fryer to 164°C. 5. Working in batches, arrange the biscuits in the air fryer basket in a single layer. Bake for about 18 minutes until the biscuits are golden brown. 6. Remove from the basket to a plate and repeat with the remaining biscuits. 7. Serve hot.

Chapter 3 Snacks and Appetisers

Crispy Green Bean Fries with Lemon-Yoghurt Sauce

Prep time: 5 minutes | Cook time: 5 minutes | Serves 4

Green Beans:
1 egg
2 tablespoons water
1 tablespoon wholemeal flour
¼ teaspoon paprika
½ teaspoon garlic powder
½ teaspoon salt
60 ml wholemeal breadcrumbs

227 g whole green beans
Lemon-Yoghurt Sauce:
120 ml non-fat plain Greek yoghurt
1 tablespoon lemon juice
¼ teaspoon salt
⅛ teaspoon cayenne pepper

Make the Green Beans: 1. Preheat the air fryer to 192°C. 2. In a medium shallow bowl, beat together the egg and water until frothy. 3. In a separate medium shallow bowl, whisk together the flour, paprika, garlic powder, and salt, then mix in the breadcrumbs. 4. Spray the bottom of the air fryer with cooking spray. 5. Dip each green bean into the egg mixture, then into the bread crumb mixture, coating the outside with the crumbs. Place the green beans in a single layer in the bottom of the air fryer basket. 6. Fry in the air fryer for 5 minutes, or until the breading is golden brown. Make the Lemon-Yoghurt Sauce: 7. In a small bowl, combine the yoghurt, lemon juice, salt, and cayenne. 8. Serve the green bean fries alongside the lemon-yoghurt sauce as a snack or appetiser.

Turkey Burger Sliders

Prep time: 10 minutes | Cook time: 5 to 7 minutes | Makes 8 sliders

450 g minced turkey
¼ teaspoon curry powder
1 teaspoon Hoisin sauce
½ teaspoon salt
8 slider rolls

120 ml slivered red onions
120 ml slivered green or red pepper
120 ml fresh chopped pineapple
Light soft white cheese

1. Combine turkey, curry powder, Hoisin sauce, and salt and mix together well. 2. Shape turkey mixture into 8 small patties. 3. Place patties in air fryer basket and air fry at 182°C for 5 to 7 minutes, until patties are well done, and juices run clear. 4. Place each patty on the bottom half of a slider roll and top with onions, peppers, and pineapple. Spread the remaining bun halves with soft white cheese to taste, place on top, and serve.

Cheesy Courgette Tots

Prep time: 15 minutes | Cook time: 6 minutes | Serves 8

2 medium courgette (about 340 g), shredded
1 large egg, whisked
120 ml grated pecorino Romano cheese

120 ml panko breadcrumbs
¼ teaspoon black pepper
1 clove garlic, minced
Cooking spray

1. Using your hands, squeeze out as much liquid from the courgette as possible. In a large bowl, mix the courgette with the remaining ingredients except the oil until well incorporated. 2. Make the courgette tots: Use a spoon or cookie scoop to place tablespoonfuls of the courgette mixture onto a lightly floured cutting board and form into 1-inch logs. 3. Preheat air fryer to 192°C. Spritz the air fryer basket with cooking spray. 4. Place the tots in the basket. You may need to cook in batches to avoid overcrowding. 5. Air fry for 6 minutes until golden brown. 6. Remove from the basket to a serving plate and repeat with the remaining courgette tots. 7. Serve immediately.

Greens Chips with Curried Yoghurt Sauce

Prep time: 10 minutes | Cook time: 5 to 6 minutes | Serves 4

240 ml low-fat Greek yoghurt
1 tablespoon freshly squeezed lemon juice
1 tablespoon curry powder
½ bunch curly kale, stemmed, ribs removed and discarded,

leaves cut into 2- to 3-inch pieces
½ bunch chard, stemmed, ribs removed and discarded, leaves cut into 2- to 3-inch pieces
1½ teaspoons olive oil

1. In a small bowl, stir together the yoghurt, lemon juice, and curry powder. Set aside. 2. In a large bowl, toss the kale and chard with the olive oil, working the oil into the leaves with your hands. This helps break up the fibres in the leaves so the chips are tender. 3. Air fry the greens in batches at 200°C for 5 to 6 minutes, until crisp, shaking the basket once during cooking. Serve with the yoghurt sauce.

Homemade Sweet Potato Chips

Prep time: 5 minutes | Cook time: 15 minutes | Serves 2

1 large sweet potato, sliced thin
⅛ teaspoon salt
2 tablespoons olive oil

1. Preheat the air fryer to 192°C. 2. In a small bowl, toss the sweet potatoes, salt, and olive oil together until the potatoes are well coated. 3. Put the sweet potato slices into the air fryer and spread them out in a single layer. 4. Fry for 10 minutes. Stir, then air fry for 3 to 5 minutes more, or until the chips reach the preferred level of crispiness.

Air Fryer Popcorn with Garlic Salt

Prep time: 3 minutes | Cook time: 10 minutes | Serves 2

2 tablespoons olive oil
60 ml popcorn kernels
1 teaspoon garlic salt

1. Preheat the air fryer to 192°C. 2. Tear a square of aluminium foil the size of the bottom of the air fryer and place into the air fryer. 3. Drizzle olive oil over the top of the foil, and then pour in the popcorn kernels. 4. Roast for 8 to 10 minutes, or until the popcorn stops popping. 5. Transfer the popcorn to a large bowl and sprinkle with garlic salt before serving.

Lebanese Muhammara

Prep time: 15 minutes | Cook time: 15 minutes | Serves 6

2 large red peppers
60 ml plus 2 tablespoons extra-virgin olive oil
240 ml walnut halves
1 tablespoon agave nectar or honey
1 teaspoon fresh lemon juice
1 teaspoon ground cumin
1 teaspoon rock salt
1 teaspoon red pepper flakes
Raw vegetables (such as cucumber, carrots, courgette slices, or cauliflower) or toasted pitta chips, for serving

1. Drizzle the peppers with 2 tablespoons of the olive oil and place in the air fryer basket. Set the air fryer to 204°C for 10 minutes. 2. Add the walnuts to the basket, arranging them around the peppers. Set the air fryer to 204°C for 5 minutes. 3. Remove the peppers, seal in a resealable plastic bag, and let rest for 5 to 10 minutes. Transfer the walnuts to a plate and set aside to cool. 4. Place the softened peppers, walnuts, agave, lemon juice, cumin, salt, and ½ teaspoon of the pepper flakes in a food processor and purée until smooth. 5. Transfer the dip to a serving bowl and make an indentation in the middle. Pour the remaining 60 ml olive oil into the indentation. Garnish the dip with the remaining ½ teaspoon pepper flakes. 6. Serve with vegetables or toasted pitta chips.

Shrimp Toasts with Sesame Seeds

Prep time: 15 minutes | Cook time: 6 to 8 minutes | Serves 4 to 6

230 g raw shrimp, peeled and deveined
1 egg, beaten
2 spring onions, chopped, plus more for garnish
2 tablespoons chopped fresh coriander
2 teaspoons grated fresh ginger
1 to 2 teaspoons sriracha sauce
1 teaspoon soy sauce
½ teaspoon toasted sesame oil
6 slices thinly sliced white sandwich bread
120 ml sesame seeds
Cooking spray
Thai chilli sauce, for serving

1. Preheat the air fryer to 204°C. Spritz the air fryer basket with cooking spray. 2. In a food processor, add the shrimp, egg, spring onions, coriander, ginger, sriracha sauce, soy sauce and sesame oil, and pulse until chopped finely. You'll need to stop the food processor occasionally to scrape down the sides. Transfer the shrimp mixture to a bowl. 3. On a clean work surface, cut the crusts off the sandwich bread. Using a brush, generously brush one side of each slice of bread with shrimp mixture. 4. Place the sesame seeds on a plate. Press bread slices, shrimp-side down, into sesame seeds to coat evenly. Cut each slice diagonally into quarters. 5. Spread the coated slices in a single layer in the air fryer basket. 6. Air fry in batches for 6 to 8 minutes, or until golden and crispy. Flip the bread slices halfway through. Repeat with the remaining bread slices. 7. Transfer to a plate and let cool for 5 minutes. Top with the chopped spring onions and serve warm with Thai chilli sauce.

Old Bay Chicken Wings

Prep time: 10 minutes | Cook time: 12 to 15 minutes | Serves 4

2 tablespoons Old Bay or all-purpose seasoning
2 teaspoons baking powder
2 teaspoons salt
900 g chicken wings, patted dry
Cooking spray

1. Preheat the air fryer to 204°C. Lightly spray the air fryer basket with cooking spray. 2. Combine the seasoning, baking powder, and salt in a large zip-top plastic bag. Add the chicken wings, seal, and shake until the wings are thoroughly coated in the seasoning mixture. 3. Lay the chicken wings in the air fryer basket in a single layer and lightly mist with cooking spray. You may need to work in batches to avoid overcrowding. 4. Air fry for 12 to 15 minutes, flipping the wings halfway through, or until the wings are lightly browned and the internal temperature reaches at least 74°C on a meat thermometer. 5. Remove from the basket to a plate and repeat with the remaining chicken wings. 6. Serve hot.

Crispy Mozzarella Sticks

Prep time: 8 minutes | Cook time: 5 minutes | Serves 4

120 ml plain flour	½ teaspoon garlic salt
1 egg, beaten	6 Mozzarella sticks, halved
120 ml panko breadcrumbs	crosswise
120 ml grated Parmesan cheese	Olive oil spray
1 teaspoon Italian seasoning	

1. Put the flour in a small bowl. 2. Put the beaten egg in another small bowl. 3. In a medium bowl, stir together the panko, Parmesan cheese, Italian seasoning, and garlic salt. 4. Roll a Mozzarella-stick half in the flour, dip it into the egg, and then roll it in the panko mixture to coat. Press the coating lightly to make sure the breadcrumbs stick to the cheese. Repeat with the remaining 11 Mozzarella sticks. 5. Insert the crisper plate into the basket and the basket into the unit. Preheat the unit by selecting AIR FRY, setting the temperature to 204ºC, and setting the time to 3 minutes. Select START/STOP to begin. 6. Once the unit is preheated, spray the crisper plate with olive oil and place a parchment paper liner in the basket. Place the Mozzarella sticks into the basket and lightly spray them with olive oil. 7. Select AIR FRY, set the temperature to 204ºC, and set the time to 5 minutes. Select START/STOP to begin. 8. When the cooking is complete, the Mozzarella sticks should be golden and crispy. Let the sticks stand for 1 minute before transferring them to a serving plate. Serve warm.

Pork and Cabbage Egg Rolls

Prep time: 15 minutes | Cook time: 12 minutes | Makes 12 egg rolls

Cooking oil spray	ginger
2 garlic cloves, minced	475 ml shredded green cabbage
340 g minced pork	4 spring onions, green parts
1 teaspoon sesame oil	(white parts optional), chopped
60 ml soy sauce	24 egg roll wrappers
2 teaspoons grated peeled fresh	

1. Spray a skillet with the cooking oil and place it over medium-high heat. Add the garlic and cook for 1 minute until fragrant. 2. Add the minced pork to the skillet. Using a spoon, break the pork into smaller chunks. 3. In a small bowl, whisk the sesame oil, soy sauce, and ginger until combined. Add the sauce to the skillet. Stir to combine and continue cooking for about 5 minutes until the pork is browned and thoroughly cooked. 4. Stir in the cabbage and spring onions. Transfer the pork mixture to a large bowl. 5. Lay the egg roll wrappers on a flat surface. Dip a basting brush in water and glaze each egg roll wrapper along the edges with the wet brush. This will soften the dough and make it easier to roll. 6. Stack 2 egg roll wrappers (it works best if you double-wrap the egg rolls).

Scoop 1 to 2 tablespoons of the pork mixture into the centre of each wrapper stack. 7. Roll one long side of the wrappers up over the filling. Press firmly on the area with the filling, tucking it in lightly to secure it in place. Fold in the left and right sides. Continue rolling to close. Use the basting brush to wet the seam and seal the egg roll. Repeat with the remaining ingredients. 8. Insert the crisper plate into the basket and the basket into the unit. Preheat the unit by selecting AIR FRY, setting the temperature to 204ºC, and setting the time to 3 minutes. Select START/STOP to begin. 9. Once the unit is preheated, spray the crisper plate with cooking oil. Place the egg rolls into the basket. It is okay to stack them. Spray them with cooking oil. 10. Select AIR FRY, set the temperature to 204ºC, and set the time to 12 minutes. Insert the basket into the unit. Select START/STOP to begin. 11. After 8 minutes, use tongs to flip the egg rolls. Reinsert the basket to resume cooking. 12. When the cooking is complete, serve the egg rolls hot.

Mexican Potato Skins

Prep time: 10 minutes | Cook time: 55 minutes | Serves 6

Olive oil	beans
6 medium russet or Maris Piper	1 tablespoon taco seasoning
potatoes, scrubbed	120 ml salsa
Salt and freshly ground black	177 ml low-fat shredded
pepper, to taste	Cheddar cheese
240 ml fat-free refried black	

1. Spray the air fryer basket lightly with olive oil. 2. Spray the potatoes lightly with oil and season with salt and pepper. Pierce each potato a few times with a fork. 3. Place the potatoes in the air fryer basket. Air fry at 204ºC until fork-tender, 30 to 40 minutes. The cooking time will depend on the size of the potatoes. You can cook the potatoes in the microwave or a standard oven, but they won't get the same lovely crispy skin they will get in the air fryer. 4. While the potatoes are cooking, in a small bowl, mix together the beans and taco seasoning. Set aside until the potatoes are cool enough to handle. 5. Cut each potato in half lengthwise. Scoop out most of the insides, leaving about ¼ inch in the skins so the potato skins hold their shape. 6. Season the insides of the potato skins with salt and black pepper. Lightly spray the insides of the potato skins with oil. You may need to cook them in batches. 7. Place them into the air fryer basket, skin-side down, and air fry until crisp and golden, 8 to 10 minutes. 8. Transfer the skins to a work surface and spoon ½ tablespoon of seasoned refried black beans into each one. Top each with 2 teaspoons salsa and 1 tablespoon shredded Cheddar cheese. 9. Place filled potato skins in the air fryer basket in a single layer. Lightly spray with oil. 10. Air fry until the cheese is melted and bubbly, 2 to 3 minutes.

Polenta Fries with Chilli-Lime Mayo

Prep time: 10 minutes | Cook time: 28 minutes | Serves 4

Polenta Fries:
2 teaspoons vegetable or olive oil
¼ teaspoon paprika
450 g prepared polenta, cut into 3-inch × ½-inch strips
Chilli-Lime Mayo:
120 ml mayonnaise

1 teaspoon chilli powder
1 teaspoon chopped fresh coriander
¼ teaspoon ground cumin
Juice of ½ lime
Salt and freshly ground black pepper, to taste

1. Preheat the air fryer to 204ºC. 2. Mix the oil and paprika in a bowl. Add the polenta strips and toss until evenly coated. 3. Transfer the polenta strips to the air fry basket and air fry for 28 minutes until the fries are golden brown, shaking the basket once during cooking. Season as desired with salt and pepper. 4. Meanwhile, whisk together all the ingredients for the chilli-lime mayo in a small bowl. 5. Remove the polenta fries from the air fryer to a plate and serve alongside the chilli-lime mayo as a dipping sauce.

Golden Onion Rings

Prep time: 15 minutes | Cook time: 14 minutes per batch | Serves 4

1 large white onion, peeled and cut into ½ to ¾-inch-thick slices (about 475 ml)
120 ml semi-skimmed milk
240 ml wholemeal pastry flour, or plain flour
2 tablespoons cornflour
¾ teaspoon sea salt, divided
½ teaspoon freshly ground

black pepper, divided
¾ teaspoon granulated garlic, divided
355 ml wholemeal breadcrumbs, or gluten-free breadcrumbs
Cooking oil spray (coconut, sunflower, or safflower)
Ketchup, for serving (optional)

1. Carefully separate the onion slices into rings—a gentle touch is important here. 2. Place the milk in a shallow bowl and set aside. 3. Make the first breading: In a medium bowl, stir together the flour, cornflour, ¼ teaspoon of salt, ¼ teaspoon of pepper, and ¼ teaspoon of granulated garlic. Set aside. 4. Make the second breading: In a separate medium bowl, stir together the breadcrumbs with the remaining ½ teaspoon of salt, the remaining ½ teaspoon of garlic, and the remaining ½ teaspoon of pepper. Set aside. 5. Insert the crisper plate into the basket and the basket into the unit. Preheat the unit by selecting AIR FRY, setting the temperature to 200ºC, and setting the time to 3 minutes. Select START/STOP to begin. 6. Once the unit is preheated, spray the crisper plate and the basket with cooking oil. 7. To make the onion rings, dip one ring into the milk and into the first breading mixture. Dip the ring into the milk again and back into the first breading mixture, coating thoroughly.

Dip the ring into the milk one last time and then into the second breading mixture, coating thoroughly. Gently lay the onion ring in the basket. Repeat with additional rings and, as you place them into the basket, do not overlap them too much. Once all the onion rings are in the basket, generously spray the tops with cooking oil. 8. Select AIR FRY, set the temperature to 200ºC, and set the time to 14 minutes. Insert the basket into the unit. Select START/STOP to begin. 9. After 4 minutes, open the unit and spray the rings generously with cooking oil. Close the unit to resume cooking. After 3 minutes, remove the basket and spray the onion rings again. Remove the rings, turn them over, and place them back into the basket. Generously spray them again with oil. Reinsert the basket to resume cooking. After 4 minutes, generously spray the rings with oil one last time. Resume cooking for the remaining 3 minutes, or until the onion rings are very crunchy and brown. 10. When the cooking is complete, serve the hot rings with ketchup, or other sauce of choice.

Crispy Chilli Chickpeas

Prep time: 5 minutes | Cook time: 15 minutes | Serves 4

1 (425 g) can cooked chickpeas, drained and rinsed
1 tablespoon olive oil
¼ teaspoon salt

⅛ teaspoon chilli powder
⅛ teaspoon garlic powder
⅛ teaspoon paprika

1. Preheat the air fryer to 192ºC. 2. In a medium bowl, toss all of the ingredients together until the chickpeas are well coated. 3. Pour the chickpeas into the air fryer and spread them out in a single layer. 4. Roast for 15 minutes, stirring once halfway through the cook time.

Jalapeño Poppers

Prep time: 10 minutes | Cook time: 20 minutes | Serves 4

Oil, for spraying
227 g soft white cheese
177 ml gluten-free breadcrumbs, divided
2 tablespoons chopped fresh

parsley
½ teaspoon granulated garlic
½ teaspoon salt
10 jalapeño peppers, halved and seeded

1. Line the air fryer basket with parchment and spray lightly with oil. 2. In a medium bowl, mix together the soft white cheese, half of the breadcrumbs, the parsley, garlic, and salt. 3. Spoon the mixture into the jalapeño halves. Gently press the stuffed jalapeños in the remaining breadcrumbs. 4. Place the stuffed jalapeños in the prepared basket. 5. Air fry at 188ºC for 20 minutes, or until the cheese is melted and the breadcrumbs are crisp and golden brown.

Five-Ingredient Falafel with Garlic-Yoghurt Sauce

Prep time: 5 minutes | Cook time: 15 minutes | Serves 4

Falafel:	Salt
1 (425 g) can chickpeas, drained and rinsed	Garlic-Yoghurt Sauce:
120 ml fresh parsley	240 ml non-fat plain Greek yoghurt
2 garlic cloves, minced	1 garlic clove, minced
½ tablespoon ground cumin	1 tablespoon chopped fresh dill
1 tablespoon wholemeal flour	2 tablespoons lemon juice

Make the Falafel: 1. Preheat the air fryer to 182°C. 2. Put the chickpeas into a food processor. Pulse until mostly chopped, then add the parsley, garlic, and cumin and pulse for another 1 to 2 minutes, or until the ingredients are combined and turning into a dough. 3. Add the flour. Pulse a few more times until combined. The dough will have texture, but the chickpeas should be pulsed into small bits. 4. Using clean hands, roll the dough into 8 balls of equal size, then pat the balls down a bit so they are about ½-thick disks. 5. Spray the basket of the air fryer with olive oil cooking spray, then place the falafel patties in the basket in a single layer, making sure they don't touch each other. 6. Fry in the air fryer for 15 minutes. Make the garlic-yoghurt sauce 7. In a small bowl, combine the yoghurt, garlic, dill, and lemon juice. 8. Once the falafel is done cooking and nicely browned on all sides, remove them from the air fryer and season with salt. 9. Serve hot with a side of dipping sauce.

Roasted Pearl Onion Dip

Prep time: 5 minutes | Cook time: 12 minutes | Serves 4

475 ml peeled pearl onions	1 tablespoon lemon juice
3 garlic cloves	¼ teaspoon black pepper
3 tablespoons olive oil, divided	⅛ teaspoon red pepper flakes
½ teaspoon salt	Pitta chips, vegetables, or
240 ml non-fat plain Greek yoghurt	toasted bread for serving (optional)

1. Preheat the air fryer to 182°C. 2. In a large bowl, combine the pearl onions and garlic with 2 tablespoons of the olive oil until the onions are well coated. 3. Pour the garlic-and-onion mixture into the air fryer basket and roast for 12 minutes. 4. Transfer the garlic and onions to a food processor. Pulse the vegetables several times, until the onions are minced but still have some chunks. 5. In a large bowl, combine the garlic and onions and the remaining 1 tablespoon of olive oil, along with the salt, yoghurt, lemon juice, black pepper, and red pepper flakes. 6. Cover and chill for 1 hour before serving with pitta chips, vegetables, or toasted bread.

Garlicky and Cheesy French Fries

Prep time: 5 minutes | Cook time: 20 to 25 minutes | Serves 4

3 medium russet or Maris Piper potatoes, rinsed, dried, and cut into thin wedges or classic fry shapes	80 ml grated Parmesan cheese
	½ teaspoon salt
	¼ teaspoon freshly ground black pepper
2 tablespoons extra-virgin olive oil	Cooking oil spray
1 tablespoon granulated garlic	2 tablespoons finely chopped fresh parsley (optional)

1. In a large bowl combine the potato wedges or fries and the olive oil. Toss to coat. 2. Sprinkle the potatoes with the granulated garlic, Parmesan cheese, salt, and pepper, and toss again. 3. Insert the crisper plate into the basket and the basket into the unit. Preheat the unit by selecting AIR FRY, setting the temperature to 204°C, and setting the time to 3 minutes. Select START/STOP to begin. 4. Once the unit is preheated, spray the crisper plate with cooking oil. Place the potatoes into the basket. 5. Select AIR FRY, set the temperature to 204°C, and set the time to 20 to 25 minutes. Select START/STOP to begin. 6. After about 10 minutes, remove the basket and shake it so the fries at the bottom come up to the top. Reinsert the basket to resume cooking. 7. When the cooking is complete, top the fries with the parsley (if using) and serve hot.

Egg Roll Pizza Sticks

Prep time: 10 minutes | Cook time: 5 minutes | Serves 4

Olive oil	24 slices turkey pepperoni or salami
8 pieces low-fat string cheese	
8 egg roll wrappers or spring roll pastry	Marinara sauce, for dipping (optional)

1. Spray the air fryer basket lightly with olive oil. Fill a small bowl with water. 2. Place each egg roll wrapper diagonally on a work surface. It should look like a diamond. 3. Place 3 slices of turkey pepperoni in a vertical line down the centre of the wrapper. 4. Place 1 Mozzarella cheese stick on top of the turkey pepperoni. 5. Fold the top and bottom corners of the egg roll wrapper over the cheese stick. 6. Fold the left corner over the cheese stick and roll the cheese stick up to resemble a spring roll. Dip a finger in the water and seal the edge of the roll 7. Repeat with the rest of the pizza sticks. 8. Place them in the air fryer basket in a single layer, making sure to leave a little space between each one. Lightly spray the pizza sticks with oil. You may need to cook these in batches. 9. Air fry at 192°C until the pizza sticks are lightly browned and crispy, about 5 minutes. 10. These are best served hot while the cheese is melted. Accompany with a small bowl of marinara sauce, if desired.

Chilli-Brined Fried Calamari

Prep time: 20 minutes | Cook time: 8 minutes | Serves 2

1 (227 g) jar sweet or hot pickled cherry peppers
227 g calamari bodies and tentacles, bodies cut into ½-inch-wide rings
1 lemon
475 ml plain flour
Rock salt and freshly ground
black pepper, to taste
3 large eggs, lightly beaten
Cooking spray
120 ml mayonnaise
1 teaspoon finely chopped rosemary
1 garlic clove, minced

1. Drain the pickled pepper brine into a large bowl and tear the peppers into bite-size strips. Add the pepper strips and calamari to the brine and let stand in the refrigerator for 20 minutes or up to 2 hours. 2. Grate the lemon zest into a large bowl then whisk in the flour and season with salt and pepper. Dip the calamari and pepper strips in the egg, then toss them in the flour mixture until fully coated. Spray the calamari and peppers liberally with cooking spray, then transfer half to the air fryer. Air fry at 204ºC, shaking the basket halfway into cooking, until the calamari is cooked through and golden brown, about 8 minutes. Transfer to a plate and repeat with the remaining pieces. 3. In a small bowl, whisk together the mayonnaise, rosemary, and garlic. Squeeze half the zested lemon to get 1 tablespoon of juice and stir it into the sauce. Season with salt and pepper. Cut the remaining zested lemon half into 4 small wedges and serve alongside the calamari, peppers, and sauce.

Italian Rice Balls

Prep time: 20 minutes | Cook time: 10 minutes | Makes 8 rice balls

355 ml cooked sticky rice
½ teaspoon Italian seasoning blend
¾ teaspoon salt, divided
8 black olives, pitted
28 g Mozzarella cheese, cut
into tiny pieces (small enough to stuff into olives)
2 eggs
80 ml Italian breadcrumbs
177 ml panko breadcrumbs
Cooking spray

1. Preheat air fryer to 200ºC. 2. Stuff each black olive with a piece of Mozzarella cheese. Set aside. 3. In a bowl, combine the cooked sticky rice, Italian seasoning blend, and ½ teaspoon of salt and stir to mix well. Form the rice mixture into a log with your hands and divide it into 8 equal portions. Mould each portion around a black olive and roll into a ball. 4. Transfer to the freezer to chill for 10 to 15 minutes until firm. 5. In a shallow dish, place the Italian breadcrumbs. In a separate shallow dish, whisk the eggs. In a third shallow dish, combine the panko breadcrumbs and remaining salt. 6. One by one, roll the rice balls in the Italian breadcrumbs, then dip in the whisked eggs, finally coat them with the panko breadcrumbs. 7. Arrange the rice balls in the air fryer basket and spritz both sides

with cooking spray. 8. Air fry for 10 minutes until the rice balls are golden brown. Flip the balls halfway through the cooking time. 9. Serve warm.

Peppery Chicken Meatballs

Prep time: 5 minutes | Cook time: 13 to 20 minutes | Makes 16 meatballs

2 teaspoons olive oil
60 ml minced onion
60 ml minced red pepper
2 vanilla wafers, crushed
1 egg white
½ teaspoon dried thyme
230 g minced chicken breast

1. Preheat the air fryer to 188ºC. 2. In a baking pan, mix the olive oil, onion, and red pepper. Put the pan in the air fryer. Air fry for 3 to 5 minutes, or until the vegetables are tender. 3. In a medium bowl, mix the cooked vegetables, crushed wafers, egg white, and thyme until well combined 4. Mix in the chicken, gently but thoroughly, until everything is combined. 5. Form the mixture into 16 meatballs and place them in the air fryer basket. Air fry for 10 to 15 minutes, or until the meatballs reach an internal temperature of 74ºC on a meat thermometer. 6. Serve immediately.

Parmesan French Fries

Prep time: 10 minutes | Cook time: 15 minutes per batch | Serves 2

2 to 3 large russet or Maris Piper potatoes, peeled and cut into ½-inch sticks
2 teaspoons vegetable or rapeseed oil
177 ml grated Parmesan cheese
½ teaspoon salt
Freshly ground black pepper, to taste
1 teaspoon fresh chopped parsley

1. Bring a large saucepan of salted water to a boil on the stovetop while you peel and cut the potatoes. Blanch the potatoes in the boiling salted water for 4 minutes while you preheat the air fryer to 204ºC. Strain the potatoes and rinse them with cold water. Dry them well with a clean kitchen towel. 2. Toss the dried potato sticks gently with the oil and place them in the air fryer basket. Air fry for 25 minutes, shaking the basket a few times while the fries cook to help them brown evenly. 3. Combine the Parmesan cheese, salt and pepper. With 2 minutes left on the air fryer cooking time, sprinkle the fries with the Parmesan cheese mixture. Toss the fries to coat them evenly with the cheese mixture and continue to air fry for the final 2 minutes, until the cheese has melted and just starts to brown. Sprinkle the finished fries with chopped parsley, a little more grated Parmesan cheese if you like, and serve.

Cheesy Steak Fries

Prep time: 5 minutes | Cook time: 20 minutes | Serves 5

1 (794 g) bag frozen steak fries	240 ml shredded Mozzarella
Cooking spray	cheese
Salt and pepper, to taste	2 spring onions, green parts
120 ml beef gravy	only, chopped

1. Preheat the air fryer to 204°C. 2. Place the frozen steak fries in the air fryer. Air fry for 10 minutes. Shake the basket and spritz the fries with cooking spray. Sprinkle with salt and pepper. Air fry for an additional 8 minutes. 3. Pour the beef gravy into a medium, microwave-safe bowl. Microwave for 30 seconds, or until the gravy is warm. 4. Sprinkle the fries with the cheese. Air fry for an additional 2 minutes, until the cheese is melted. 5. Transfer the fries to a serving dish. Drizzle the fries with gravy and sprinkle the spring onions on top for a green garnish. Serve.

Root Veggie Chips with Herb Salt

Prep time: 10 minutes | Cook time: 8 minutes | Serves 2

1 parsnip, washed	Cooking spray
1 small beetroot, washed	Herb Salt:
1 small turnip, washed	¼ teaspoon rock salt
½ small sweet potato, washed	2 teaspoons finely chopped
1 teaspoon olive oil	fresh parsley

1. Preheat the air fryer to 182°C. 2. Peel and thinly slice the parsnip, beetroot, turnip, and sweet potato, then place the vegetables in a large bowl, add the olive oil, and toss. 3. Spray the air fryer basket with cooking spray, then place the vegetables in the basket and air fry for 8 minutes, gently shaking the basket halfway through. 4. While the chips cook, make the herb salt in a small bowl by combining the rock salt and parsley. 5. Remove the chips and place on a serving plate, then sprinkle the herb salt on top and allow to cool for 2 to 3 minutes before serving.

Roasted Grape Dip

Prep time: 10 minutes | Cook time: 8 to 12 minutes | Serves 6

475 ml seedless red grapes,	240 ml low-fat Greek yoghurt
rinsed and patted dry	2 tablespoons semi-skimmed
1 tablespoon apple cider	milk
vinegar	2 tablespoons minced fresh
1 tablespoon honey	basil

1. In the air fryer basket, sprinkle the grapes with the cider vinegar and drizzle with the honey. Toss to coat. Roast the grapes at 192°C for 8 to 12 minutes, or until shrivelled but still soft. Remove from the air fryer. 2. In a medium bowl, stir together the yoghurt and milk. 3. Gently blend in the grapes and basil. Serve immediately or cover and chill for 1 to 2 hours.

Onion Pakoras

Prep time: 30 minutes | Cook time: 10 minutes per batch | Serves 2

2 medium brown or white	tablespoons chickpea flour
onions, sliced (475 ml)	1 teaspoon ground turmeric
120 ml chopped fresh coriander	1 teaspoon cumin seeds
2 tablespoons vegetable oil	1 teaspoon rock salt
1 tablespoon chickpea flour	½ teaspoon cayenne pepper
1 tablespoon rice flour, or 2	Vegetable oil spray

1. In a large bowl, combine the onions, coriander, oil, chickpea flour, rice flour, turmeric, cumin seeds, salt, and cayenne. Stir to combine. Cover and let stand for 30 minutes or up to overnight. (This allows the onions to release moisture, creating a batter.) Mix well before using. 2. Spray the air fryer basket generously with vegetable oil spray. Drop half of the batter in 6 heaping tablespoons into the basket. Set the air fryer to 176°C for 8 minutes. Carefully turn the pakoras over and spray with oil spray. Set the air fryer for 2 minutes, or until the batter is cooked through and crisp. 3. Repeat with remaining batter to make 6 more pakoras, checking at 6 minutes for doneness. Serve hot.

Soft white cheese Stuffed Jalapeño Poppers

Prep time: 12 minutes | Cook time: 6 to 8 minutes | Serves 10

227 g soft white cheese, at	minced
room temperature	1 teaspoon chilli powder
240 ml panko breadcrumbs,	10 jalapeño peppers, halved and
divided	seeded
2 tablespoons fresh parsley,	Cooking oil spray

1. In a small bowl, whisk the soft white cheese, 120 ml of panko, the parsley, and chilli powder until combined. Stuff the cheese mixture into the jalapeño halves. 2. Sprinkle the tops of the stuffed jalapeños with the remaining 120 ml of panko and press it lightly into the filling. 3. Insert the crisper plate into the basket and the basket into the unit. Preheat the unit by selecting AIR FRY, setting the temperature to 192°C, and setting the time to 3 minutes. Select START/STOP to begin. 4. Once the unit is preheated, spray the crisper plate with cooking oil. Place the poppers into the basket. 5. Select AIR FRY, set the temperature to 192°C, and set the time to 8 minutes. Select START/STOP to begin. 6. After 6 minutes, check the poppers. If they are softened and the cheese is melted, they are done. If not, resume cooking. 7. When the cooking is complete, serve warm.

Kale Chips with Tex-Mex Dip

240 ml Greek yoghurt

1 tablespoon chilli powder

80 ml low-salt salsa, well drained

1 bunch curly kale

1 teaspoon olive oil

¼ teaspoon coarse sea salt

1. In a small bowl, combine the yoghurt, chilli powder, and drained salsa; refrigerate. 2. Rinse the kale thoroughly, and pat dry. Remove the stems and ribs from the kale, using a sharp knife. Cut or tear the leaves into 3-inch pieces. 3. Toss the kale with the olive oil in a large bowl. 4. Air fry the kale in small batches at 200ºC until the leaves are crisp. This should take 5 to 6 minutes. Shake the basket once during cooking time. 5. As you remove the kale chips, sprinkle them with a bit of the sea salt. 6. When all of the kale chips are done, serve with the dip.

Chapter 4 Pizzas, Wraps, and Sandwiches

Buffalo Chicken French Bread Pizza

Prep time: 10 minutes | Cook time: 12 minutes | Serves 8

Oil, for spraying
1 loaf French bread, cut in half and split lengthwise
4 tablespoons unsalted butter, melted
475 ml shredded or diced rotisserie chicken
110 g soft white cheese

3 tablespoons buffalo sauce, plus more for serving
2 tablespoons dry ranch seasoning
475 ml shredded Mozzarella cheese
80 ml crumbled blue cheese

1.Line the air fryer basket with parchment and spray lightly with oil. Brush the cut sides of the bread with the melted butter. 2. Place the bread in the prepared basket. You may need to work in batches, depending on the size of your air fryer. Air fry at 204ºC for 5 to 7 minutes, or until the bread is toasted. 3. In a medium bowl, mix together the chicken, soft white cheese, buffalo sauce, and ranch seasoning. 4. Divide the mixture equally among the toasted bread and spread in an even layer. Top with the Mozzarella cheese and blue cheese and cook for another 3 to 5 minutes, or until the cheese is melted. 5. Let cool for 2 to 3 minutes before cutting into 2-inch slices. Serve with additional buffalo sauce for drizzling.

Turkish Pizza

Prep time: 20 minutes | Cook time: 10 minutes | Serves 4

110 g minced lamb or 15% fat minced beef
60 ml finely chopped green pepper
60 ml chopped fresh parsley
1 small plum tomato, seeded and finely chopped
2 tablespoons finely chopped brown onion
1 garlic clove, minced
2 teaspoons tomato paste
¼ teaspoon sweet paprika

¼ teaspoon ground cumin
⅛ to ¼ teaspoon red pepper flakes
⅛ teaspoon ground allspice
⅛ teaspoon rock salt
⅛ teaspoon black pepper
4 (6-inch) flour tortillas
For Serving:
Chopped fresh mint
Extra-virgin olive oil
Lemon wedges

1.In a medium bowl, gently mix the lamb, pepper, parsley, chopped tomato, onion, garlic, tomato paste, paprika, cumin, red pepper flakes, allspice, salt, and black pepper until well combined. 2. Divide the meat mixture evenly among the tortillas, spreading it all the way to the edge of each tortilla. 3. Place 1 tortilla in the air fryer basket. Set the air fryer to 204ºC for 10 minutes, or until the meat topping has browned and the edge of the tortilla is golden. 4. Transfer to a plate and repeat to cook the remaining tortillas. Serve the pizzas warm, topped with chopped fresh mint and a drizzle of extra-virgin olive oil and with lemon wedges alongside.

Turkey-Hummus Wraps

Prep time: 10 minutes | Cook time: 3 to 7 minutes per batch | Serves 4

4 large wholemeal wraps
120 ml hummus
16 thin slices deli turkey

8 slices provolone cheese
235 ml fresh baby spinach (or more to taste)

1.To assemble, place 2 tablespoons of hummus on each wrap and spread to within about a half inch from edges. Top with 4 slices of turkey and 2 slices of provolone. Finish with 60 ml baby spinach or pile on as much as you like. Roll up each wrap. You don't need to fold or seal the ends. 2. Place 2 wraps in air fryer basket, seam side down. Air fry at 182ºC for 3 to 4 minutes to warm filling and melt cheese. If you like, you can continue cooking for 2 or 3 more minutes, until the wrap is slightly crispy. Repeat step 4 to cook remaining wraps.

Vegetable Pitta Sandwiches

Prep time: 15 minutes | Cook time: 9 to 12 minutes | Serves 4

1 baby aubergine, peeled and chopped
1 red pepper, sliced
120 ml diced red onion
120 ml shredded carrot

1 teaspoon olive oil
80 ml low-fat Greek yoghurt
½ teaspoon dried tarragon
2 low-salt wholemeal pitta breads, halved crosswise

1.In a baking pan, stir together the aubergine, red pepper, red onion, carrot, and olive oil. Put the vegetable mixture into the air fryer basket and roast at 200ºC for 7 to 9 minutes, stirring once, until the vegetables are tender. 2. Drain if necessary. In a small bowl, thoroughly mix the yoghurt and tarragon until well combined. Stir the yoghurt mixture into the vegetables. Stuff one-fourth of this mixture into each pitta pocket. 3. Place the sandwiches in the air fryer and cook for 2 to 3 minutes, or until the bread is toasted. Serve immediately.

Golden Cod Tacos with Salsa

Prep time: 5 minutes | Cook time: 15 minutes | Serves 4

2 eggs
300 ml Mexican beer
350 ml coconut flour
350 ml almond flour
½ tablespoon chilli powder
1 tablespoon cumin
Salt, to taste

450 g cod fillet, sliced into large
pieces
4 toasted corn tortillas
4 large lettuce leaves, chopped
60 ml salsa
Cooking spray

1.Preheat the air fryer to 192ºC. 2. Spritz the air fryer basket with cooking spray. 3. Break the eggs in a bowl, then pour in the beer. Whisk to combine well. Combine the coconut flour, almond flour, chilli powder, cumin, and salt in a separate bowl. Stir to mix well. 4. Dunk the cod pieces in the egg mixture, then shake the excess off and dredge into the flour mixture to coat well. 5. Arrange the cod in the preheated air fryer. Air fry for 15 minutes or until golden brown. Flip the cod halfway through the cooking time. 6. Unwrap the toasted tortillas on a large plate, then divide the cod and lettuce leaves on top. Baste with salsa and wrap to serve.

Avocado and Slaw Tacos

Prep time: 15 minutes | Cook time: 6 minutes | Serves 4

60 ml plain flour
¼ teaspoon salt, plus more as
needed
¼ teaspoon ground black
pepper
2 large egg whites
300 ml panko breadcrumbs
2 tablespoons olive oil
2 avocados, peeled and halved,
cut into ½-inch-thick slices
½ small red cabbage, thinly

sliced
1 deseeded jalapeño, thinly
sliced
2 spring onions, thinly sliced
120 ml coriander leaves
60 ml mayonnaise
Juice and zest of 1 lime
4 corn tortillas, warmed
120 ml sour cream
Cooking spray

1.Preheat the air fryer to 204ºC. 2. Spritz the air fryer basket with cooking spray. 3. Pour the flour in a large bowl and sprinkle with salt and black pepper, then stir to mix well. 4. Whisk the egg whites in a separate bowl. Combine the panko with olive oil on a shallow dish. Dredge the avocado slices in the bowl of flour, then into the egg to coat. Shake the excess off, then roll the slices over the panko. 5. Arrange the avocado slices in a single layer in the basket and spritz the cooking spray. Air fry for 6 minutes or until tender and lightly browned. Flip the slices halfway through with tongs. Combine the cabbage, jalapeño, onions, coriander leaves, mayo, lime juice and zest, and a touch of salt in a separate large bowl. Toss to mix well. 6. Unfold the tortillas on a clean work surface, then spread with cabbage slaw and air fried avocados. Top with sour cream and serve.

Shrimp and Grilled Cheese Sandwiches

Prep time: 10 minutes | Cook time: 5 minutes | Serves 4

300 ml shredded Colby,
Cheddar, or Havarti cheese
1 (170 g) can tiny shrimp,
drained
3 tablespoons mayonnaise

2 tablespoons minced spring
onion
4 slices wholemeal or
wholemeal bread
2 tablespoons softened butter

1.In a medium bowl, combine the cheese, shrimp, mayonnaise, and spring onion, and mix well. 2. Spread this mixture on two of the slices of bread. Top with the other slices of bread to make two sandwiches. Spread the sandwiches lightly with butter. 3. Air fry at 204ºC for 5 to 7 minutes or until the bread is browned and crisp and the cheese is melted. 4. Cut in half and serve warm.

Mediterranean-Pitta Wraps

Prep time: 5 minutes | Cook time: 14 minutes | Serves 4

450 g mackerel fish fillets
2 tablespoons olive oil
1 tablespoon Mediterranean
seasoning mix
½ teaspoon chilli powder

Sea salt and freshly ground
black pepper, to taste
60 g feta cheese, crumbled
4 tortillas

1.Toss the fish fillets with the olive oil; place them in the lightly oiled air fryer basket. 2. Air fry the fish fillets at 204ºC for about 14 minutes, turning them over halfway through the cooking time. 3. Assemble your pittas with the chopped fish and remaining ingredients and serve warm.

Air Fried Soft white cheese Wontons

Prep time: 5 minutes | Cook time: 6 minutes | Serves 4

60 g soft white cheese, softened
1 tablespoon sugar
16 square wonton or egg roll

wrappers
Cooking spray

1.Preheat the air fryer to 176ºC. Spritz the air fryer basket with cooking spray. 2. In a mixing bowl, stir together the soft white cheese and sugar until well mixed. Prepare a small bowl of water alongside. 3. On a clean work surface, lay the wonton wrappers. Scoop ¼ teaspoon of soft white cheese in the centre of each wonton wrapper. Dab the water over the wrapper edges. Fold each wonton wrapper diagonally in half over the filling to form a triangle. 4. Arrange the wontons in the air fryer basket. Spritz the wontons with cooking spray. Air fry for 6 minutes, or until golden brown and crispy. Flip once halfway through to ensure even cooking. 5. Divide the wontons among four plates. 6. Let rest for 5 minutes before serving.

Grilled Cheese Sandwich

Prep time: 5 minutes | Cook time: 5 minutes | Makes 2 sandwiches

4 slices bread

110 g Cheddar cheese slices

2 teaspoons butter or oil

1.Lay the four cheese slices on two of the bread slices and top with the remaining two slices of bread. 2. Brush both sides with butter or oil and cut the sandwiches in rectangular halves. 3. Place in air fryer basket and air fry at 200ºC for 5 minutes until the outside is crisp and the cheese melts.

Tuna Wraps

Prep time: 10 minutes | Cook time: 4 to 7 minutes | Serves 4

450 g fresh tuna steak, cut into 1-inch cubes

1 tablespoon grated fresh ginger

2 garlic cloves, minced

½ teaspoon toasted sesame oil

4 low-salt wholemeal tortillas

60 ml low-fat mayonnaise

475 ml shredded romaine lettuce

1 red pepper, thinly sliced

1.In a medium bowl, mix the tuna, ginger, garlic, and sesame oil. Let it stand for 10 minutes. 2. Air fry the tuna in the air fryer at 200ºC for 4 to 7 minutes, or until done to your liking and lightly browned. 3. Make wraps with the tuna, tortillas, mayonnaise, lettuce, and pepper. 4. Serve immediately.

Crispy Chicken Egg Rolls

Prep time: 10 minutes | Cook time: 23 to 24 minutes | Serves 4

450 g minced chicken

2 teaspoons olive oil

2 garlic cloves, minced

1 teaspoon grated fresh ginger

475 ml white cabbage, shredded

1 onion, chopped

60 ml soy sauce

8 egg roll wrappers

1 egg, beaten

Cooking spray

1.Preheat the air fryer to 188ºC. 2. Spritz the air fryer basket with cooking spray. 3. Heat olive oil in a saucepan over medium heat. Sauté the garlic and ginger in the olive oil for 1 minute, or until fragrant. Add the minced chicken to the saucepan. Sauté for 5 minutes, or until the chicken is cooked through. Add the cabbage, onion and soy sauce and sauté for 5 to 6 minutes, or until the vegetables become soft. Remove the saucepan from the heat. 4. Unfold the egg roll wrappers on a clean work surface. Divide the chicken mixture among the wrappers and brush the edges of the wrappers with the beaten egg. Tightly roll up the egg rolls,

enclosing the filling. 5. Arrange the rolls in the prepared air fryer basket and air fry for 12 minutes, or until crispy and golden brown. Turn halfway through the cooking time to ensure even cooking. 6. Transfer to a platter and let cool for 5 minutes before serving.

Beef and Pepper Fajitas

Prep time: 15 minutes | Cook time: 10 minutes | Serves 4

450 g beef sirloin steak, cut into strips

2 shallots, sliced

1 orange pepper, sliced

1 red pepper, sliced

2 garlic cloves, minced

2 tablespoons Cajun seasoning

1 tablespoon paprika

Salt and ground black pepper, to taste

4 corn tortillas

120 ml shredded Cheddar cheese

Cooking spray

1.Preheat the air fryer to 182ºC and spritz with cooking spray. 2. Combine all the ingredients, except for the tortillas and cheese, in a large bowl. Toss to coat well. 3. Pour the beef and vegetables in the preheated air fryer and spritz with cooking spray. Air fry for 10 minutes or until the meat is browned and the vegetables are soft and lightly wilted. Shake the basket halfway through. 4. Unfold the tortillas on a clean work surface and spread the cooked beef and vegetables on top. 5. Scatter with cheese and fold to serve.

Jerk Chicken Wraps

Prep time: 30 minutes | Cook time: 15 minutes | Serves 4

450 g boneless, skinless chicken tenderloins

235 ml jerk marinade

Olive oil

4 large low-carb tortillas

235 ml julienned carrots

235 ml peeled cucumber ribbons

235 ml shredded lettuce

235 ml mango or pineapple chunks

1.In a medium bowl, coat the chicken with the jerk marinade, cover, and refrigerate for 1 hour. 2. Spray the air fryer basket lightly with olive oil. Place the chicken in the air fryer basket in a single layer and spray lightly with olive oil. You may need to cook the chicken in batches. Reserve any leftover marinade. Air fry at 192ºC for 8 minutes. Turn the chicken over and brush with some of the remaining marinade. Cook until the chicken reaches an internal temperature of at least 74ºC, an additional 5 to 7 minutes. 3. To assemble the wraps, fill each tortilla with 60 ml carrots, 60 ml cucumber, 60 ml lettuce, and 60 ml mango. Place one quarter of the chicken tenderloins on top and roll up the tortilla. These are great served warm or cold.

Barbecue Chicken Pitta Pizza

Prep time: 5 minutes | Cook time: 5 to 7 minutes per batch | Makes 4 pizzas

235 ml barbecue sauce, divided
4 pitta breads
475 ml shredded cooked chicken
475 ml shredded Mozzarella

cheese
½ small red onion, thinly sliced
2 tablespoons finely chopped fresh coriander

1.Measure 120 ml of the barbecue sauce in a small measuring cup. Spread 2 tablespoons of the barbecue sauce on each pitta. 2. In a medium bowl, mix together the remaining 120 ml of barbecue sauce and chicken. Place 120 ml of the chicken on each pitta. Top each pizza with 120 ml of the Mozzarella cheese. Sprinkle the tops of the pizzas with the red onion. 3. Place one pizza in the air fryer. Air fry at 204ºC for 5 to 7 minutes. Repeat this process with the remaining pizzas. 4. Top the pizzas with the coriander.

Bacon and Pepper Sandwiches

Prep time: 15 minutes | Cook time: 7 minutes | Serves 4

80 ml spicy barbecue sauce
2 tablespoons honey
8 slices precooked bacon, cut into thirds
1 red pepper, sliced

1 yellow pepper, sliced
3 pitta pockets, cut in half
300 ml torn butterhead lettuce leaves
2 tomatoes, sliced

1.In a small bowl, combine the barbecue sauce and the honey. Brush this mixture lightly onto the bacon slices and the red and yellow pepper slices. 2. Put the peppers into the air fryer basket and air fry at 176ºC for 4 minutes. Then shake the basket, add the bacon, and air fry for 2 minutes or until the bacon is browned and the peppers are tender. 3. Fill the pitta halves with the bacon, peppers, any remaining barbecue sauce, lettuce, and tomatoes, and serve immediately.

Spinach and Ricotta Pockets

Prep time: 20 minutes | Cook time: 10 minutes per batch | Makes 8 pockets

2 large eggs, divided
1 tablespoon water
235 ml baby spinach, roughly chopped
60 ml sun-dried tomatoes, finely chopped
235 ml ricotta cheese

235 ml basil, chopped
¼ teaspoon red pepper flakes
¼ teaspoon rock salt
2 refrigerated rolled sheets of shortcrust pastry
2 tablespoons sesame seeds

1.Preheat the air fryer to 192ºC. 2. Spritz the air fryer basket with cooking spray. 3. Whisk an egg with water in a small bowl. Combine the spinach, tomatoes, the other egg, ricotta cheese, basil, red pepper flakes, and salt in a large bowl. Whisk to mix well. 4. Unfold the pastry on a clean work surface and slice each sheet into 4 wedges. Scoop up 3 tablespoons of the spinach mixture on each wedge and leave ½ inch space from edges. 5. Fold the wedges in half to wrap the filling and press the edges with a fork to seal. Arrange the wraps in the preheated air fryer and spritz with cooking spray. Sprinkle with sesame seeds. Work in 4 batches to avoid overcrowding. 6. Air fry for 10 minutes or until crispy and golden. Flip them halfway through. Serve immediately.

Mushroom Pitta Pizzas

Prep time: 10 minutes | Cook time: 5 minutes | Serves 4

4 (3-inch) pittas
1 tablespoon olive oil
180 ml pizza sauce
1 (113 g) jar sliced mushrooms, drained

½ teaspoon dried basil
2 spring onions, minced
235 ml grated Mozzarella or provolone cheese
235 ml sliced grape tomatoes

1.Brush each piece of pitta with oil and top with the pizza sauce. Add the mushrooms and sprinkle with basil and spring onions. Top with the grated cheese. 2. Bake at 182ºC for 3 to 6 minutes or until the cheese is melted and starts to brown. Top with the grape tomatoes and serve immediately.

Cheesy Spring Chicken Wraps

Prep time: 30 minutes | Cook time: 5 minutes per batch | Serves 12

2 large-sized chicken breasts, cooked and shredded
2 spring onions, chopped
284 g Ricotta cheese
1 tablespoon rice vinegar
1 tablespoon molasses
1 teaspoon grated fresh ginger

60 ml soy sauce
⅓ teaspoon sea salt
¼ teaspoon ground black pepper, or more to taste
48 wonton wrappers or egg roll wrappers
Cooking spray

1.Preheat the air fryer to 192ºC and spritz with cooking spray. 2. Combine all the ingredients, except for the wrappers in a large bowl. Toss to mix well. 3. Unfold the wrappers on a clean work surface, then divide and spoon the mixture in the middle of the wrappers. Dab a little water on the edges of the wrappers, then fold the edge close to you over the filling. Tuck the edge under the filling and roll up to seal. 4. Arrange the wraps in the preheated air fryer and air fry in batches for 5 minutes or until lightly browned. Flip the wraps halfway through. 5. Serve immediately.

Bacon Garlic Pizza

Prep time: 10 minutes | Cook time: 20 minutes | Serves 4

Flour, for dusting
Non-stick baking spray with flour
4 frozen large wholemeal bread rolls, thawed
5 cloves garlic, minced
180 ml pizza sauce

½ teaspoon dried oregano
½ teaspoon garlic salt
8 slices precooked bacon, cut into 1-inch pieces
300 ml shredded Cheddar cheese

1.On a lightly floured surface, press out each bread roll to a 5-by-3-inch oval. Spray four 6-by-4-inch pieces of heavy-duty foil with non-stick spray and place one crust on each piece. 2. Bake, two at a time, at 188°C for 2 minutes or until the crusts are set, but not browned. Meanwhile, in a small bowl, combine the garlic, pizza sauce, oregano, and garlic salt. When the pizza crusts are set, spread each with some of the sauce. Top with the bacon pieces and Cheddar cheese. Bake, two at a time, for another 8 minutes or until the crust is browned and the cheese is melted and starting to brown.

Chapter 5 Poultry

Thanksgiving Turkey Breast

Prep time: 5 minutes | Cook time: 30 minutes | Serves 4

1½ teaspoons fine sea salt

1 teaspoon ground black pepper

1 teaspoon chopped fresh rosemary leaves

1 teaspoon chopped fresh sage

1 teaspoon chopped fresh tarragon

1 teaspoon chopped fresh thyme leaves

1 (900 g) turkey breast

3 tablespoons ghee or unsalted butter, melted

3 tablespoons Dijon mustard

1. Spray the air fryer with avocado oil. Preheat the air fryer to 200ºC. 2. In a small bowl, stir together the salt, pepper, and herbs until well combined. Season the turkey breast generously on all sides with the seasoning. 3. In another small bowl, stir together the ghee and Dijon. Brush the ghee mixture on all sides of the turkey breast. 4. Place the turkey breast in the air fryer basket and air fry for 30 minutes, or until the internal temperature reaches 76ºC. Transfer the breast to a cutting board and allow it to rest for 10 minutes before cutting it into ½-inch-thick slices. 5. Store leftovers in an airtight container in the refrigerator for up to 4 days or in the freezer for up to a month. Reheat in a preheated 180ºC air fryer for 4 minutes, or until warmed through.

Tex-Mex Chicken Roll-Ups

Prep time: 10 minutes | Cook time: 14 to 17 minutes | Serves 8

900 g boneless, skinless chicken breasts or thighs

1 teaspoon chili powder

½ teaspoon smoked paprika

½ teaspoon ground cumin

Sea salt and freshly ground

black pepper, to taste

170 g Monterey Jack cheese, shredded

115 g canned diced green chilies

Avocado oil spray

1. Place the chicken in a large zip-top bag or between two pieces of plastic wrap. Using a meat mallet or heavy skillet, pound the chicken until it is about ¼ inch thick. 2. In a small bowl, combine the chili powder, smoked paprika, cumin, and salt and pepper to taste. Sprinkle both sides of the chicken with the seasonings. 3. Sprinkle the chicken with the Monterey Jack cheese, then the diced green chilies. 4. Roll up each piece of chicken from the long side, tucking in the ends as you go. Secure the roll-up with a toothpick. 5. Set the air fryer to 180ºC. . Spray the outside of the chicken with avocado oil. Place the chicken in a single layer in the basket, working in batches if necessary, and roast for 7 minutes. Flip and cook for another 7 to 10 minutes, until an instant-read thermometer reads 70ºC. 6. Remove the chicken from the air fryer and allow it to rest for about 5 minutes before serving.

Thai Tacos with Peanut Sauce

Prep time: 10 minutes | Cook time: 6 minutes | Serves 4

450 g chicken mince

10 g diced onions (about 1 small onion)

2 cloves garlic, minced

¼ teaspoon fine sea salt

Sauce:

60 g creamy peanut butter, room temperature

2 tablespoons chicken broth, plus more if needed

2 tablespoons lime juice

2 tablespoons grated fresh ginger

2 tablespoons wheat-free tamari or coconut aminos

1½ teaspoons hot sauce

5 drops liquid stevia (optional)

For Serving:

2 small heads butter lettuce, leaves separated

Lime slices (optional)

For Garnish (Optional):

Coriander leaves

Shredded purple cabbage

Sliced green onions

1. Preheat the air fryer to 180ºC. . 2. Place the chicken mince, onions, garlic, and salt in a pie pan or a dish that will fit in your air fryer. Break up the chicken with a spatula. Place in the air fryer and bake for 5 minutes, or until the chicken is browned and cooked through. Break up the chicken again into small crumbles. 3. Make the sauce: In a medium-sized bowl, stir together the peanut butter, broth, lime juice, ginger, tamari, hot sauce, and stevia (if using) until well combined. If the sauce is too thick, add another tablespoon or two of broth. Taste and add more hot sauce if desired. 4. Add half of the sauce to the pan with the chicken. Cook for another minute, until heated through, and stir well to combine. 5. Assemble the tacos: Place several lettuce leaves on a serving plate. Place a few tablespoons of the chicken mixture in each lettuce leaf and garnish with coriander leaves, purple cabbage, and sliced green onions, if desired. Serve the remaining sauce on the side. Serve with lime slices, if desired. 6. Store leftover meat mixture in an airtight container in the refrigerator for up to 4 days; store leftover sauce, lettuce leaves, and garnishes separately. Reheat the meat mixture in a lightly greased pie pan in a preheated 180ºC air fryer for 3 minutes, or until heated through.

Classic Chicken Kebab

Prep time: 35 minutes | Cook time: 25 minutes | Serves 4

60 ml olive oil
1 teaspoon garlic powder
1 teaspoon onion powder
1 teaspoon ground cumin
½ teaspoon dried oregano
½ teaspoon dried basil
60 ml lemon juice
1 tablespoon apple cider vinegar
Olive oil cooking spray

450 g boneless skinless chicken thighs, cut into 1-inch pieces
1 red bell pepper, cut into 1-inch pieces
1 red onion, cut into 1-inch pieces
1 courgette, cut into 1-inch pieces
12 cherry tomatoes

1. In a large bowl, mix together the olive oil, garlic powder, onion powder, cumin, oregano, basil, lemon juice, and apple cider vinegar. 2. Spray six skewers with olive oil cooking spray. 3. On each skewer, slide on a piece of chicken, then a piece of bell pepper, onion, courgette, and finally a tomato and then repeat. Each skewer should have at least two pieces of each item. 4. Once all of the skewers are prepared, place them in a 9-by-13-inch baking dish and pour the olive oil marinade over the top of the skewers. Turn each skewer so that all sides of the chicken and vegetables are coated. 5. Cover the dish with plastic wrap and place it in the refrigerator for 30 minutes. 6. After 30 minutes, preheat the air fryer to 192°C. (If using a grill attachment, make sure it is inside the air fryer during preheating.) 7. Remove the skewers from the marinade and lay them in a single layer in the air fryer basket. If the air fryer has a grill attachment, you can also lay them on this instead. 8. Cook for 10 minutes. Rotate the kebabs, then cook them for 15 minutes more. 9. Remove the skewers from the air fryer and let them rest for 5 minutes before serving.

Almond-Crusted Chicken

Prep time: 15 minutes | Cook time: 25 minutes | Serves 4

20 g slivered almonds
2 (170 g) boneless, skinless chicken breasts

2 tablespoons full-fat mayonnaise
1 tablespoon Dijon mustard

1. Pulse the almonds in a food processor or chop until finely chopped. Place almonds evenly on a plate and set aside. 2. Completely slice each chicken breast in half lengthwise. 3. Mix the mayonnaise and mustard in a small bowl and then coat chicken with the mixture. 4. Lay each piece of chicken in the chopped almonds to fully coat. Carefully move the pieces into the air fryer basket. 5. Adjust the temperature to 180°C and air fry for 25 minutes. 6. Chicken will be done when it has reached an internal temperature of 76°C or more. Serve warm.

Golden Chicken Cutlets

Prep time: 15 minutes | Cook time: 15 minutes | Serves 4

2 tablespoons panko breadcrumbs
20 g grated Parmesan cheese
⅛ tablespoon paprika
½ tablespoon garlic powder
2 large eggs

4 chicken cutlets
1 tablespoon parsley
Salt and ground black pepper, to taste
Cooking spray

1. Preheat air fryer to 200°C. Spritz the air fryer basket with cooking spray. 2. Combine the breadcrumbs, Parmesan, paprika, garlic powder, salt, and ground black pepper in a large bowl. Stir to mix well. Beat the eggs in a separate bowl. 3. Dredge the chicken cutlets in the beaten eggs, then roll over the breadcrumbs mixture to coat well. Shake the excess off. 4. Transfer the chicken cutlets in the preheated air fryer and spritz with cooking spray. 5. Air fry for 15 minutes or until crispy and golden brown. Flip the cutlets halfway through. 6. Serve with parsley on top.

Chicken Paillard

Prep time: 10 minutes | Cook time: 10 minutes | Serves 2

2 large eggs, room temperature
1 tablespoon water
40 g powdered Parmesan cheese or pork dust
2 teaspoons dried thyme leaves
1 teaspoon ground black pepper
2 (140 g) boneless, skinless chicken breasts, pounded to ½ inch thick

Lemon Butter Sauce:
2 tablespoons unsalted butter, melted
2 teaspoons lemon juice
¼ teaspoon finely chopped fresh thyme leaves, plus more for garnish
⅛ teaspoon fine sea salt
Lemon slices, for serving

1. Spray the air fryer basket with avocado oil. Preheat the air fryer to 200°C. 2. Beat the eggs in a shallow dish, then add the water and stir well. 3. In a separate shallow dish, mix together the Parmesan, thyme, and pepper until well combined. 4. One at a time, dip the chicken breasts in the eggs and let any excess drip off, then dredge both sides of the chicken in the Parmesan mixture. As you finish, set the coated chicken in the air fryer basket. 5. Roast the chicken in the air fryer for 5 minutes, then flip the chicken and cook for another 5 minutes, or until cooked through and the internal temperature reaches 76°C. 6. While the chicken cooks, make the lemon butter sauce: In a small bowl, mix together all the sauce ingredients until well combined. 7. Plate the chicken and pour the sauce over it. Garnish with chopped fresh thyme and serve with lemon slices. 8. Store leftovers in an airtight container in the refrigerator for up to 4 days. Reheat in a preheated 200°C air fryer for 5 minutes, or until heated through.

Ethiopian Chicken with Cauliflower

Prep time: 15 minutes | Cook time: 28 minutes | Serves 6

2 handful fresh Italian parsley, roughly chopped
20 g fresh chopped chives
2 sprigs thyme
6 chicken drumsticks
1½ small-sized head cauliflower, broken into large-sized florets
2 teaspoons mustard powder
⅓ teaspoon porcini powder
1½ teaspoons berbere spice
⅓ teaspoon sweet paprika
½ teaspoon shallot powder
1teaspoon granulated garlic
1 teaspoon freshly cracked pink peppercorns
½ teaspoon sea salt

1. Simply combine all items for the berbere spice rub mix. After that, coat the chicken drumsticks with this rub mix on all sides. Transfer them to the baking dish. 2. Now, lower the cauliflower onto the chicken drumsticks. Add thyme, chives and Italian parsley and spritz everything with a pan spray. Transfer the baking dish to the preheated air fryer. 3. Next step, set the timer for 28 minutes; roast at 180ºC, turning occasionally. Bon appétit!

Coriander Chicken Kebabs

Prep time: 30 minutes | Cook time: 10 minutes | Serves 4

Chutney:
40 g unsweetened shredded coconut
120 ml hot water
40 g fresh coriander leaves, roughly chopped
10 g fresh mint leaves, roughly chopped
6 cloves garlic, roughly
chopped
1 jalapeño, seeded and roughly chopped
60-75 ml water, as needed
Juice of 1 lemon
Chicken:
450 g boneless, skinless chicken thighs, cut crosswise into thirds
Olive oil spray

1. For the chutney: In a blender or food processor, combine the coconut and hot water; set aside to soak for 5 minutes. 2. To the processor, add the coriander, mint, garlic, and jalapeño, along with 60 ml water. Blend at low speed, stopping occasionally to scrape down the sides. Add the lemon juice. With the blender or processor running, add only enough additional water to keep the contents moving. Turn the blender to high once the contents are moving freely and blend until the mixture is puréed. 3. For the chicken: Place the chicken pieces in a large bowl. Add ¼ cup of the chutney and mix well to coat. Set aside the remaining chutney to use as a dip. Marinate the chicken for 15 minutes at room temperature. 4. Spray the air fryer basket with olive oil spray. Arrange the chicken in the air fryer basket. Set the air fryer to 180ºC for 10 minutes. Use a meat thermometer to ensure that the chicken has reached an internal temperature of 76ºC. 5. Serve the chicken with the remaining chutney.

Thai-Style Cornish Game Hens

Prep time: 30 minutes | Cook time: 20 minutes | Serves 4

20 g chopped fresh coriander leaves and stems
60 ml fish sauce
1 tablespoon soy sauce
1 serrano chili, seeded and chopped
8 garlic cloves, smashed
2 tablespoons sugar
2 tablespoons lemongrass paste
2 teaspoons black pepper
2 teaspoons ground coriander
1 teaspoon kosher salt
1 teaspoon ground turmeric
2 Cornish game hens, giblets removed, split in half lengthwise

1. In a blender, combine the coriander, fish sauce, soy sauce, serrano, garlic, sugar, lemongrass, black pepper, coriander, salt, and turmeric. Blend until smooth. 2. Place the game hen halves in a large bowl. Pour the coriander mixture over the hen halves and toss to coat. Marinate at room temperature for 30 minutes, or cover and refrigerate for up to 24 hours. 3. Arrange the hen halves in a single layer in the air fryer basket. Set the air fryer to 200ºC for 20 minutes. Use a meat thermometer to ensure the game hens have reached an internal temperature of 76ºC.

Chicken Schnitzel Dogs

Prep time: 15 minutes | Cook time: 8 to 10 minutes | Serves 4

60 g flour
½ teaspoon salt
1 teaspoon marjoram
1 teaspoon dried parsley flakes
½ teaspoon thyme
1 egg
1 teaspoon lemon juice
1 teaspoon water
120 g bread crumbs
4 chicken tenders, pounded thin
Oil for misting or cooking spray
4 whole-grain hotdog buns
4 slices Gouda cheese
1 small Granny Smith apple, thinly sliced
45 g shredded Swiss Chard cabbage
Coleslaw dressing

1. In a shallow dish, mix together the flour, salt, marjoram, parsley, and thyme. 2. In another shallow dish, beat together egg, lemon juice, and water. 3. Place bread crumbs in a third shallow dish. 4. Cut each of the flattened chicken tenders in half lengthwise. 5. Dip flattened chicken strips in flour mixture, then egg wash. Let excess egg drip off and roll in bread crumbs. Spray both sides with oil or cooking spray. 6. Air fry at 200ºC for 5 minutes. Spray with oil, turn over, and spray other side. 7. Cook for 3 to 5 minutes more, until well done and crispy brown. 8. To serve, place 2 schnitzel strips on bottom of each hotdog bun. Top with cheese, sliced apple, and cabbage. Drizzle with coleslaw dressing and top with other half of bun.

Breaded Turkey Cutlets

Prep time: 5 minutes | Cook time: 8 minutes | Serves 4

60 g whole wheat bread crumbs	⅛ teaspoon garlic powder
¼ teaspoon paprika	1 egg
¼ teaspoon salt	4 turkey breast cutlets
¼ teaspoon black pepper	Chopped fresh parsley, for
⅛ teaspoon dried sage	serving

1. Preheat the air fryer to 192ºC. 2. In a medium shallow bowl, whisk together the bread crumbs, paprika, salt, black pepper, sage, and garlic powder. 3. In a separate medium shallow bowl, whisk the egg until frothy. 4. Dip each turkey cutlet into the egg mixture, then into the bread crumb mixture, coating the outside with the crumbs. Place the breaded turkey cutlets in a single layer in the bottom of the air fryer basket, making sure that they don't touch each other. 5. Bake for 4 minutes. Turn the cutlets over, then bake for 4 minutes more, or until the internal temperature reaches 76ºC. Sprinkle on the parsley and serve.

Cornish Hens with Honey-Lime Glaze

Prep time: 15 minutes | Cook time: 25 to 30 minutes | Serves 2 to 3

1 small chicken (680 to 900 g)	1 teaspoon poultry seasoning
1 tablespoon honey	Salt and pepper, to taste
1 tablespoon lime juice	Cooking spray

1. To split the chicken into halves, cut through breast bone and down one side of the backbone. 2. Mix the honey, lime juice, and poultry seasoning together and brush or rub onto all sides of the chicken. Season to taste with salt and pepper. 3. Spray the air fryer basket with cooking spray and place hen halves in the basket, skin-side down. 4. Air fry at 170ºC for 25 to 30 minutes. Chicken will be done when juices run clear when pierced at leg joint with a fork. Let chicken rest for 5 to 10 minutes before cutting.

Chicken, Courgette, and Spinach Salad

Prep time: 10 minutes | Cook time: 20 minutes | Serves 4

3 (140 g) boneless, skinless chicken breasts, cut into 1-inch cubes	1 medium red onion, sliced
	1 red bell pepper, sliced
5 teaspoons extra-virgin olive oil	1 small courgette, cut into strips
	3 tablespoons freshly squeezed lemon juice
½ teaspoon dried thyme	85 g fresh baby spinach leaves

1. Insert the crisper plate into the basket and the basket into the unit. Preheat the unit by selecting AIR ROAST, setting the temperature to 190ºC, and setting the time to 3 minutes. Select START/STOP to begin. 2. In a large bowl, combine the chicken, olive oil, and thyme. Toss to coat. Transfer to a medium metal bowl that fits into the basket. 3. Once the unit is preheated, place the bowl into the basket. 4. Select AIR ROAST, set the temperature to 190ºC, and set the time to 20 minutes. Select START/STOP to begin. 5. After 8 minutes, add the red onion, red bell pepper, and courgette to the bowl. Resume cooking. After about 6 minutes more, stir the chicken and vegetables. Resume cooking. 6. When the cooking is complete, a food thermometer inserted into the chicken should register at least 76ºC. Remove the bowl from the unit and stir in the lemon juice. 7. Put the spinach in a serving bowl and top with the chicken mixture. Toss to combine and serve immediately.

Crispy Duck with Cherry Sauce

Prep time: 10 minutes | Cook time: 33 minutes | Serves 2 to 4

1 whole duck (2.3 kg), split in half, back and rib bones removed	1 shallot, minced
	120 ml sherry
	240 g cherry preserves
1 teaspoon olive oil	240 ml chicken stock
Salt and freshly ground black pepper, to taste	1 teaspoon white wine vinegar
	1 teaspoon fresh thyme leaves
Cherry Sauce:	Salt and freshly ground black
1 tablespoon butter	pepper, to taste

1. Preheat the air fryer to 200ºC. 2. Trim some of the fat from the duck. Rub olive oil on the duck and season with salt and pepper. Place the duck halves in the air fryer basket, breast side up and facing the centre of the basket. 3. Air fry the duck for 20 minutes. Turn the duck over and air fry for another 6 minutes. 4. While duck is air frying, make the cherry sauce. Melt the butter in a large sauté pan. Add the shallot and sauté until it is just starting to brown, about 2 to 3 minutes. Add the sherry and deglaze the pan by scraping up any brown bits from the bottom of the pan. Simmer the liquid for a few minutes, until it has reduced by half. Add the cherry preserves, chicken stock and white wine vinegar. Whisk well to combine all the ingredients. Simmer the sauce until it thickens and coats the back of a spoon, about 5 to 7 minutes. Season with salt and pepper and stir in the fresh thyme leaves. 5. When the air fryer timer goes off, spoon some cherry sauce over the duck and continue to air fry at 200ºC for 4 more minutes. Then, turn the duck halves back over so that the breast side is facing up. Spoon more cherry sauce over the top of the duck, covering the skin completely. Air fry for 3 more minutes and then remove the duck to a plate to rest for a few minutes. 6. Serve the duck in halves, or cut each piece in half again for a smaller serving. Spoon any additional sauce over the duck or serve it on the side.

Porchetta-Style Chicken Breasts

Prep time: 10 minutes | Cook time: 15 minutes | Serves 4

25 g fresh parsley leaves
10 g roughly chopped fresh chives
4 cloves garlic, peeled
2 tablespoons lemon juice
3 teaspoons fine sea salt
1 teaspoon dried rubbed sage
1 teaspoon fresh rosemary leaves

1 teaspoon ground fennel
½ teaspoon red pepper flakes
4 (115 g) boneless, skinless chicken breasts, pounded to ¼ inch thick
8 slices bacon
Sprigs of fresh rosemary, for garnish (optional)

1. Spray the air fryer basket with avocado oil. Preheat the air fryer to 170°C. 2. Place the parsley, chives, garlic, lemon juice, salt, sage, rosemary, fennel, and red pepper flakes in a food processor and purée until a smooth paste forms. 3. Place the chicken breasts on a cutting board and rub the paste all over the tops. With a short end facing you, roll each breast up like a jelly roll to make a log and secure it with toothpicks. 4. Wrap 2 slices of bacon around each chicken breast log to cover the entire breast. Secure the bacon with toothpicks. 5. Place the chicken breast logs in the air fryer basket and air fry for 5 minutes, flip the logs over, and cook for another 5 minutes. Increase the heat to 200°C and cook until the bacon is crisp, about 5 minutes more. 6. Remove the toothpicks and garnish with fresh rosemary sprigs, if desired, before serving. Store leftovers in an airtight container in the refrigerator for up to 4 days or in the freezer for up to a month. Reheat in a preheated 180°C air fryer for 5 minutes, then increase the heat to 200°C and cook for 2 minutes to crisp the bacon.

Broccoli Cheese Chicken

Prep time: 15 minutes | Cook time: 25 minutes | Serves 4

1 tablespoon avocado oil
15 g chopped onion
35 g finely chopped broccoli
115 g cream cheese, at room temperature
60 g Cheddar cheese, shredded
1 teaspoon garlic powder
½ teaspoon sea salt, plus

additional for seasoning, divided
¼ freshly ground black pepper, plus additional for seasoning, divided
900 g boneless, skinless chicken breasts
1 teaspoon smoked paprika

1. Heat a medium skillet over medium-high heat and pour in the avocado oil. Add the onion and broccoli and cook, stirring occasionally, for 5 to 8 minutes, until the onion is tender. 2. Transfer to a large bowl and stir in the cream cheese, Cheddar cheese, and garlic powder, and season to taste with salt and pepper. 3. Hold a sharp knife parallel to the chicken breast and cut a long pocket into one side. Stuff the chicken pockets with the broccoli mixture, using toothpicks to secure the pockets around the filling. 4. In a small dish, combine the paprika, ½ teaspoon salt, and ¼ teaspoon pepper.

Sprinkle this over the outside of the chicken. 5. Set the air fryer to 200°C. Place the chicken in a single layer in the air fryer basket, cooking in batches if necessary, and cook for 14 to 16 minutes, until an instant-read thermometer reads 70°C. Place the chicken on a plate and tent a piece of aluminum foil over the chicken. Allow to rest for 5 to 10 minutes before serving.

Italian Flavour Chicken Breasts with Roma Tomatoes

Prep time: 10 minutes | Cook time: 60 minutes | Serves 8

1.4 kg chicken breasts, bone-in
1 teaspoon minced fresh basil
1 teaspoon minced fresh rosemary
2 tablespoons minced fresh parsley
1 teaspoon cayenne pepper

½ teaspoon salt
½ teaspoon freshly ground black pepper
4 medium Roma tomatoes, halved
Cooking spray

1. Preheat the air fryer to 190°C. Spritz the air fryer basket with cooking spray. 2. Combine all the ingredients, except for the chicken breasts and tomatoes, in a large bowl. Stir to mix well. 3. Dunk the chicken breasts in the mixture and press to coat well. 4. Transfer the chicken breasts in the preheated air fryer. You may need to work in batches to avoid overcrowding. 5. Air fry for 25 minutes or until the internal temperature of the thickest part of the breasts reaches at least 76°C. Flip the breasts halfway through the cooking time. 6. Remove the cooked chicken breasts from the basket and adjust the temperature to 180°C. 7. Place the tomatoes in the air fryer and spritz with cooking spray. Sprinkle with a touch of salt and cook for 10 minutes or until tender. Shake the basket halfway through the cooking time. 8. Serve the tomatoes with chicken breasts on a large serving plate.

Ginger Turmeric Chicken Thighs

Prep time: 5 minutes | Cook time: 25 minutes | Serves 4

4 (115 g) boneless, skin-on chicken thighs
2 tablespoons coconut oil, melted
½ teaspoon ground turmeric

½ teaspoon salt
½ teaspoon garlic powder
½ teaspoon ground ginger
¼ teaspoon ground black pepper

1. Place chicken thighs in a large bowl and drizzle with coconut oil. Sprinkle with remaining ingredients and toss to coat both sides of thighs. 2. Place thighs skin side up into ungreased air fryer basket. Adjust the temperature to 200°C and air fry for 25 minutes. After 10 minutes, turn thighs. When 5 minutes remain, flip thighs once more. Chicken will be done when skin is golden brown and the internal temperature is at least 76°C. Serve warm.

Sriracha-Honey Chicken Nuggets

Prep time: 15 minutes | Cook time: 19 minutes | Serves 6

Oil, for spraying
1 large egg
180 ml milk
125 g all-purpose flour
2 tablespoons icing sugar
½ teaspoon paprika
½ teaspoon salt

½ teaspoon freshly ground black pepper
2 boneless, skinless chicken breasts, cut into bite-size pieces
140 g barbecue sauce
2 tablespoons honey
1 tablespoon Sriracha

1. Line the air fryer basket with parchment and spray lightly with oil. 2. In a small bowl, whisk together the egg and milk. 3. In a medium bowl, combine the flour, icing sugar, paprika, salt, and black pepper and stir. 4. Coat the chicken in the egg mixture, then dredge in the flour mixture until evenly coated. 5. Place the chicken in the prepared basket and spray liberally with oil. 6. Air fry at 200°C for 8 minutes, flip, spray with more oil, and cook for another 6 to 8 minutes, or until the internal temperature reaches 76°C and the juices run clear. 7. In a large bowl, mix together the barbecue sauce, honey, and Sriracha. 8. Transfer the chicken to the bowl and toss until well coated with the barbecue sauce mixture. 9. Line the air fryer basket with fresh parchment, return the chicken to the basket, and cook for another 2 to 3 minutes, until browned and crispy.

Bacon-Wrapped Chicken Breasts Rolls

Prep time: 10 minutes | Cook time: 15 minutes | Serves 4

15 g chopped fresh chives
2 tablespoons lemon juice
1 teaspoon dried sage
1 teaspoon fresh rosemary leaves
15 g fresh parsley leaves
4 cloves garlic, peeled
1 teaspoon ground fennel
3 teaspoons sea salt

½ teaspoon red pepper flakes
4 (115 g) boneless, skinless chicken breasts, pounded to ¼ inch thick
8 slices bacon
Sprigs of fresh rosemary, for garnish
Cooking spray

1. Preheat the air fryer to 170°C. Spritz the air fryer basket with cooking spray. 2. Put the chives, lemon juice, sage, rosemary, parsley, garlic, fennel, salt, and red pepper flakes in a food processor, then pulse to purée until smooth. 3. Unfold the chicken breasts on a clean work surface, then brush the top side of the chicken breasts with the sauce. 4. Roll the chicken breasts up from the shorter side, then wrap each chicken rolls with 2 bacon slices to cover. Secure with toothpicks. 5. Arrange the rolls in the preheated air fryer, then cook for 10 minutes. Flip the rolls halfway through. 6. Increase the heat to 200°C and air fry for 5 more minutes or until the bacon is browned and crispy. 7. Transfer the rolls to a large plate. Discard the toothpicks and spread with rosemary sprigs before serving.

Crunchy Chicken Tenders

Prep time: 5 minutes | Cook time: 12 minutes | Serves 4

1 egg
60 ml unsweetened almond milk
30 g whole wheat flour
30 g whole wheat bread crumbs
½ teaspoon salt

½ teaspoon black pepper
½ teaspoon dried thyme
½ teaspoon dried sage
½ teaspoon garlic powder
450 g chicken tenderloins
1 lemon, quartered

1. Preheat the air fryer to 184°C. 2. In a shallow bowl, beat together the egg and almond milk until frothy. 3. In a separate shallow bowl, whisk together the flour, bread crumbs, salt, pepper, thyme, sage, and garlic powder. 4. Dip each chicken tenderloin into the egg mixture, then into the bread crumb mixture, coating the outside with the crumbs. Place the breaded chicken tenderloins into the bottom of the air fryer basket in an even layer, making sure that they don't touch each other. 5. Cook for 6 minutes, then turn and cook for an additional 5 to 6 minutes. Serve with lemon slices.

Buttermilk Breaded Chicken

Prep time: 7 minutes | Cook time: 20 to 25 minutes | Serves 4

125 g all-purpose flour
2 teaspoons paprika
Pinch salt
Freshly ground black pepper, to taste
80 ml buttermilk
2 eggs

2 tablespoons extra-virgin olive oil
185 g bread crumbs
6 chicken pieces, drumsticks, breasts, and thighs, patted dry
Cooking oil spray

1. In a shallow bowl, stir together the flour, paprika, salt, and pepper. 2. In another bowl, beat the buttermilk and eggs until smooth. 3. In a third bowl, stir together the olive oil and bread crumbs until mixed. 4. Dredge the chicken in the flour, dip in the eggs to coat, and finally press into the bread crumbs, patting the crumbs firmly onto the chicken skin. 5. Insert the crisper plate into the basket and the basket into the unit. Preheat the unit by selecting AIR FRY, setting the temperature to 190°C, and setting the time to 3 minutes. Select START/STOP to begin. 6. Once the unit is preheated, spray the crisper plate with cooking oil. Place the chicken into the basket. 7. Select AIR FRY, set the temperature to 190°C, and set the time to 25 minutes. Select START/STOP to begin. 8. After 10 minutes, flip the chicken. Resume cooking. After 10 minutes more, check the chicken. If a food thermometer inserted into the chicken registers 76°C and the chicken is brown and crisp, it is done. Otherwise, resume cooking for up to 5 minutes longer. 9. When the cooking is complete, let cool for 5 minutes, then serve.

Jalapeño Popper Hasselback Chicken

Prep time: 10 minutes | Cook time: 19 minutes | Serves 2

Oil, for spraying
2 (230 g) boneless, skinless chicken breasts
60 g cream cheese, softened

55 g bacon bits
20 g chopped pickled jalapeños
40 g shredded Cheddar cheese, divided

1. Line the air fryer basket with parchment and spray lightly with oil. 2. Make multiple cuts across the top of each chicken breast, cutting only halfway through. 3. In a medium bowl, mix together the cream cheese, bacon bits, jalapeños, and Cheddar cheese. Spoon some of the mixture into each cut. 4. Place the chicken in the prepared basket. 5. Air fry at 176°C for 14 minutes. Scatter the remaining cheese on top of the chicken and cook for another 2 to 5 minutes, or until the cheese is melted and the internal temperature reaches 76°C.

Butter and Bacon Chicken

Prep time: 10 minutes | Cook time: 65 minutes | Serves 6

1 (1.8 kg) whole chicken
2 tablespoons salted butter, softened
1 teaspoon dried thyme
½ teaspoon garlic powder

1 teaspoon salt
½ teaspoon ground black pepper
6 slices sugar-free bacon

1. Pat chicken dry with a paper towel, then rub with butter on all sides. Sprinkle thyme, garlic powder, salt, and pepper over chicken. 2. Place chicken into ungreased air fryer basket, breast side up. Lay strips of bacon over chicken and secure with toothpicks. 3. Adjust the temperature to 180°C and air fry for 65 minutes. Halfway through cooking, remove and set aside bacon and flip chicken over. Chicken will be done when the skin is golden and crispy and the internal temperature is at least 76°C. Serve warm with bacon.

Fajita-Stuffed Chicken Breast

Prep time: 15 minutes | Cook time: 25 minutes | Serves 4

2 (170 g) boneless, skinless chicken breasts
¼ medium white onion, peeled and sliced
1 medium green bell pepper,

seeded and sliced
1 tablespoon coconut oil
2 teaspoons chili powder
1 teaspoon ground cumin
½ teaspoon garlic powder

1. Slice each chicken breast completely in half lengthwise into two even pieces. Using a meat tenderizer, pound out the chicken until it's about ¼-inch thickness. 2. Lay each slice of chicken out and place three slices of onion and four slices of green pepper on the end closest to you. Begin rolling the peppers and onions tightly into the chicken. Secure the roll with either toothpicks or a couple

pieces of butcher's twine. 3. Drizzle coconut oil over chicken. Sprinkle each side with chili powder, cumin, and garlic powder. Place each roll into the air fryer basket. 4. Adjust the temperature to 180°C and air fry for 25 minutes. 5. Serve warm.

Bacon-Wrapped Stuffed Chicken Breasts

Prep time: 15 minutes | Cook time: 30 minutes | Serves 4

80 g chopped frozen spinach, thawed and squeezed dry
55 g cream cheese, softened
20 g grated Parmesan cheese
1 jalapeño, seeded and chopped
½ teaspoon kosher salt
1 teaspoon black pepper

2 large boneless, skinless chicken breasts, butterflied and pounded to ½-inch thickness
4 teaspoons salt-free Cajun seasoning
6 slices bacon

1. In a small bowl, combine the spinach, cream cheese, Parmesan cheese, jalapeño, salt, and pepper. Stir until well combined. 2. Place the butterflied chicken breasts on a flat surface. Spread the cream cheese mixture evenly across each piece of chicken. Starting with the narrow end, roll up each chicken breast, ensuring the filling stays inside. Season chicken with the Cajun seasoning, patting it in to ensure it sticks to the meat. 3. Wrap each breast in 3 slices of bacon. Place in the air fryer basket. Set the air fryer to 180°C for 30 minutes. Use a meat thermometer to ensure the chicken has reached an internal temperature of 76°C. 4. Let the chicken stand 5 minutes before slicing each rolled-up breast in half to serve.

Bruschetta Chicken

Prep time: 10 minutes | Cook time: 20 minutes | Serves 4

Bruschetta Stuffing:
1 tomato, diced
3 tablespoons balsamic vinegar
1 teaspoon Italian seasoning
2 tablespoons chopped fresh basil
3 garlic cloves, minced
2 tablespoons extra-virgin olive

oil
Chicken:
4 (115 g) boneless, skinless chicken breasts, cut 4 slits each
1 teaspoon Italian seasoning
Chicken seasoning or rub, to taste
Cooking spray

1. Preheat the air fryer to 190°. Spritz the air fryer basket with cooking spray. 2. Combine the ingredients for the bruschetta stuffing in a bowl. Stir to mix well. Set aside. 3. Rub the chicken breasts with Italian seasoning and chicken seasoning on a clean work surface. 4. Arrange the chicken breasts, slits side up, in a single layer in the air fryer basket and spritz with cooking spray. You may need to work in batches to avoid overcrowding. 5. Air fry for 7 minutes, then open the air fryer and fill the slits in the chicken with the bruschetta stuffing. Cook for another 3 minutes or until the chicken is well browned. 6. Serve immediately.

Fried Chicken Breasts

Prep time: 30 minutes | Cook time: 12 to 14 minutes | Serves 4

450 g boneless, skinless chicken breasts	cheese
180 ml dill pickle juice	½ teaspoon sea salt
70 g finely ground blanched almond flour	½ teaspoon freshly ground black pepper
70 g finely grated Parmesan	2 large eggs
	Avocado oil spray

1. Place the chicken breasts in a zip-top bag or between two pieces of plastic wrap. Using a meat mallet or heavy skillet, pound the chicken to a uniform ½-inch thickness. 2. Place the chicken in a large bowl with the pickle juice. Cover and allow to brine in the refrigerator for up to 2 hours. 3. In a shallow dish, combine the almond flour, Parmesan cheese, salt, and pepper. In a separate, shallow bowl, beat the eggs. 4. Drain the chicken and pat it dry with paper towels. Dip in the eggs and then in the flour mixture, making sure to press the coating into the chicken. Spray both sides of the coated breasts with oil. 5. Spray the air fryer basket with oil and put the chicken inside. Set the temperature to 200ºC and air fry for 6 to 7 minutes. 6. Carefully flip the breasts with a spatula. Spray the breasts again with oil and continue cooking for 6 to 7 minutes more, until golden and crispy.

Chicken Hand Pies

Prep time: 30 minutes | Cook time: 10 minutes per batch | Makes 8 pies

180 ml chicken broth	1 tablespoon milk
130 g frozen mixed peas and carrots	Salt and pepper, to taste
140 g cooked chicken, chopped	1 (8-count) can organic flaky biscuits
1 tablespoon cornflour	Oil for misting or cooking spray

1. In a medium saucepan, bring chicken broth to a boil. Stir in the frozen peas and carrots and cook for 5 minutes over medium heat. Stir in chicken. 2. Mix the cornflour into the milk until it dissolves. Stir it into the simmering chicken broth mixture and cook just until thickened. 3. Remove from heat, add salt and pepper to taste, and let cool slightly. 4. Lay biscuits out on wax paper. Peel each biscuit apart in the middle to make 2 rounds so you have 16 rounds total. Using your hands or a rolling pin, flatten each biscuit round slightly to make it larger and thinner. 5. Divide chicken filling among 8 of the biscuit rounds. Place remaining biscuit rounds on top and press edges all around. Use the tines of a fork to crimp biscuit edges and make sure they are sealed well. 6. Spray both sides lightly with oil or cooking spray. 7. Cook in a single layer, 4 at a time, at 170ºC for 10 minutes or until biscuit dough is cooked through and golden brown.

Sweet and Spicy Turkey Meatballs

Prep time: 15 minutes | Cook time: 15 minutes | Serves 6

Olive oil	sauce, divided
450 g lean turkey mince	2 teaspoons minced garlic
60 g whole-wheat panko bread crumbs	⅛ teaspoon salt
1 egg, beaten	⅛ teaspoon freshly ground black pepper
1 tablespoon soy sauce	1 teaspoon Sriracha
60 ml plus 1 tablespoon hoisin	

1. Spray the air fryer basket lightly with olive oil. 2. In a large bowl, mix together the turkey, panko bread crumbs, egg, soy sauce, 1 tablespoon of hoisin sauce, garlic, salt, and black pepper. 3. Using a tablespoon, form 24 meatballs. 4. In a small bowl, combine the remaining 60 ml of hoisin sauce and Sriracha to make a glaze and set aside. 5. Place the meatballs in the air fryer basket in a single layer. You may need to cook them in batches. 6. Air fry at 180ºC for 8 minutes. Brush the meatballs generously with the glaze and cook until cooked through, an additional 4 to 7 minutes.

Apricot-Glazed Chicken Drumsticks

Prep time: 15 minutes | Cook time: 30 minutes | Makes 6 drumsticks

For the Glaze:	6 chicken drumsticks
160 g apricot preserves	½ teaspoon seasoning salt
½ teaspoon tamari	1 teaspoon salt
¼ teaspoon chili powder	½ teaspoon ground black
2 teaspoons Dijon mustard	pepper
For the Chicken:	Cooking spray

Make the glaze: 1. Combine the ingredients for the glaze in a saucepan, then heat over low heat for 10 minutes or until thickened. 2. Turn off the heat and sit until ready to use. Make the Chicken: 1. Preheat the air fryer to 190ºC. Spritz the air fryer basket with cooking spray. 2. Combine the seasoning salt, salt, and pepper in a small bowl. Stir to mix well. 3. Place the chicken drumsticks in the preheated air fryer. Spritz with cooking spray and sprinkle with the salt mixture on both sides. 4. Air fry for 20 minutes or until well browned. Flip the chicken halfway through. 5. Baste the chicken with the glaze and air fryer for 2 more minutes or until the chicken tenderloin is glossy. 6. Serve immediately.

Quick Chicken Fajitas

Prep time: 10 minutes | Cook time: 15 minutes | Serves 2

280 g boneless, skinless chicken breast, sliced into ¼-inch strips
2 tablespoons coconut oil, melted
1 tablespoon chili powder
½ teaspoon cumin
½ teaspoon paprika

½ teaspoon garlic powder
¼ medium onion, peeled and sliced
½ medium green bell pepper, seeded and sliced
½ medium red bell pepper, seeded and sliced

1. Place chicken and coconut oil into a large bowl and sprinkle with chili powder, cumin, paprika, and garlic powder. Toss chicken until well coated with seasoning. Place chicken into the air fryer basket. 2. Adjust the temperature to 180°C and air fry for 15 minutes. 3. Add onion and peppers into the basket when the cooking time has 7 minutes remaining. 4. Toss the chicken two or three times during cooking. Vegetables should be tender and chicken fully cooked to at least 76°C internal temperature when finished. Serve warm.

Fajita Chicken Strips

Prep time: 10 minutes | Cook time: 15 minutes | Serves 4

450 g boneless, skinless chicken tenderloins, cut into strips
3 bell peppers, any color, cut into chunks
1 onion, cut into chunks

1 tablespoon olive oil
1 tablespoon fajita seasoning mix
Cooking spray

1. Preheat the air fryer to 190°C. 2. In a large bowl, mix together the chicken, bell peppers, onion, olive oil, and fajita seasoning mix until completely coated. 3. Spray the air fryer basket lightly with cooking spray. 4. Place the chicken and vegetables in the air fryer basket and lightly spray with cooking spray. 5. Air fry for 7 minutes. Shake the basket and air fry for an additional 5 to 8 minutes, until the chicken is cooked through and the veggies are starting to char. 6. Serve warm.

Chicken Schnitzel

Prep time: 15 minutes | Cook time: 5 minutes | Serves 4

60 g all-purpose flour
1 teaspoon marjoram
½ teaspoon thyme
1 teaspoon dried parsley flakes
½ teaspoon salt
1 egg

1 teaspoon lemon juice
1 teaspoon water
120 g breadcrumbs
4 chicken tenders, pounded thin, cut in half lengthwise
Cooking spray

1. Preheat the air fryer to 200°C and spritz with cooking spray. 2. Combine the flour, marjoram, thyme, parsley, and salt in a shallow dish. Stir to mix well. 3. Whisk the egg with lemon juice and water in a large bowl. Pour the breadcrumbs in a separate shallow dish. 4. Roll the chicken halves in the flour mixture first, then in the egg mixture, and then roll over the breadcrumbs to coat well. Shake the excess off. 5. Arrange the chicken halves in the preheated air fryer and spritz with cooking spray on both sides. 6. Air fry for 5 minutes or until the chicken halves are golden brown and crispy. Flip the halves halfway through. 7. Serve immediately.

Chapter 6 Beef, Pork, and Lamb

Bulgogi Burgers

Prep time: 30 minutes | Cook time: 10 minutes | Serves 4

Burgers:
450 g 85% lean beef mince
60 ml chopped spring onionspring onions
2 tablespoons gochujang (Korean red chili paste)
1 tablespoon dark soy sauce
2 teaspoons minced garlic
2 teaspoons minced fresh ginger
2 teaspoons sugar
1 tablespoon toasted sesame oil
½ teaspoon coarse or flaky salt
Gochujang Mayonnaise:
60 ml mayonnaise
60 ml chopped spring onionspring onions
1 tablespoon gochujang (Korean red chili paste)
1 tablespoon toasted sesame oil
2 teaspoons sesame seeds
4 hamburger buns

1. For the burgers: In a large bowl, mix the ground beef, spring onionspring onions, gochujang, soy sauce, garlic, ginger, sugar, sesame oil, and salt. Marinate at room temperature for 30 minutes, or cover and refrigerate for up to 24 hours. 2. Divide the meat into four portions and form them into round patties. Make a slight depression in the middle of each patty with your thumb to prevent them from puffing up into a dome shape while cooking. 3. Place the patties in a single layer in the air fryer basket. Set the air fryer to 176ºC for 10 minutes. 4. Meanwhile, for the gochujang mayonnaise: Stir together the mayonnaise, spring onionspring onions, gochujang, sesame oil, and sesame seeds. 5. At the end of the cooking time, use a meat thermometer to ensure the burgers have reached an internal temperature of 72ºC (medium). 6. To serve, place the burgers on the buns and top with the mayonnaise.

Spicy Rump Steak

Prep time: 25 minutes | Cook time: 12 to 18 minutes | Serves 4

2 tablespoons salsa
1 tablespoon minced chipotle pepper or chipotle paste
1 tablespoon apple cider vinegar
1 teaspoon ground cumin
⅛ teaspoon freshly ground
black pepper
⅛ teaspoon red pepper flakes
340 g rump steak, cut into 4 pieces and gently pounded to about ⅓ inch thick
Cooking oil spray

1. In a small bowl, thoroughly mix the salsa, chipotle pepper, vinegar, cumin, black pepper, and red pepper flakes. Rub this mixture into both sides of each steak piece. Let stand for 15 minutes at room temperature. 2. Insert the crisper plate into the basket and place the basket into the unit. Preheat the unit by selecting AIR FRY, setting the temperature to 200ºC, and setting the time to 3 minutes. Select START/STOP to begin. 3. Once the unit is preheated, spray the crisper plate with cooking oil. Working in batches, place 2 steaks into the basket. 4. Select AIR FRY, set the temperature to 200ºC, and set the time to 9 minutes. Select START/STOP to begin. 5. After about 6 minutes, check the steaks. If a food thermometer inserted into the meat registers at least 64ºC, they are done. If not, resume cooking. 6. When the cooking is done, transfer the steaks to a clean plate and cover with aluminum foil to keep warm. Repeat steps 3, 4, and 5 with the remaining steaks. 7. Thinly slice the steaks against the grain and serve.

Greek Lamb Pitta Pockets

Prep time: 15 minutes | Cook time: 6 minutes | Serves 4

Dressing:
235 ml plain yogurt
1 tablespoon lemon juice
1 teaspoon dried dill, crushed
1 teaspoon ground oregano
½ teaspoon salt
Meatballs:
230 g lamb mince
1 tablespoon diced onion
1 teaspoon dried parsley
1 teaspoon dried dill, crushed
¼ teaspoon oregano
¼ teaspoon coriander
¼ teaspoon ground cumin
¼ teaspoon salt
4 pitta halves
Suggested Toppings:
1 red onion, slivered
1 medium cucumber, deseeded, thinly sliced
Crumbled feta cheese
Sliced black olives
Chopped fresh peppers

1. Preheat the air fryer to 200ºC. 2. Stir the dressing ingredients together in a small bowl and refrigerate while preparing lamb. 3. Combine all meatball ingredients in a large bowl and stir to distribute seasonings. 4. Shape meat mixture into 12 small meatballs, rounded or slightly flattened if you prefer. 5. Transfer the meatballs in the preheated air fryer and air fry for 6 minutes, until well done. Remove and drain on paper towels. 6. To serve, pile meatballs and the choice of toppings in pitta pockets and drizzle with dressing.

Steak, Broccoli, and Mushroom Rice Bowls

Prep time: 10 minutes | Cook time: 15 to 18 minutes | Serves 4

2 tablespoons cornflour	1 onion, chopped
120 ml low-sodium beef stock	235 ml sliced white or chestnut
1 teaspoon reduced-salt soy	mushrooms
sauce	1 tablespoon grated peeled
340 g rump steak, cut into	fresh ginger
1-inch cubes	Cooked brown rice (optional),
120 ml broccoli florets	for serving

1. In a medium bowl, stir together the cornflour, beef stock, and soy sauce until the cornflour is completely dissolved. 2. Add the beef cubes and toss to coat. Let stand for 5 minutes at room temperature. 3. Insert the crisper plate into the basket and the basket into the unit. Preheat the unit by selecting AIR FRY, setting the temperature to 204°C, and setting the time to 3 minutes. Select START/STOP to begin. 4. Once the unit is preheated, use a slotted spoon to transfer the beef from the stock mixture into a medium metal bowl that fits into the basket. Reserve the stock. Add the broccoli, onion, mushrooms, and ginger to the beef. Place the bowl into the basket. 5. Select AIR FRY, set the temperature to 204°C, and set the time to 18 minutes. Select START/STOP to begin. 6. After about 12 minutes, check the beef and broccoli. If a food thermometer inserted into the beef registers at least 64°C and the vegetables are tender, add the reserved stock and resume cooking for about 3 minutes until the sauce boils. If not, resume cooking for about 3 minutes before adding the reservedstock. 7. When the cooking is complete, serve immediately over hot cooked brown rice, if desired.

Stuffed Beef Fillet with Feta Cheese

Prep time: 10 minutes | Cook time: 10 minutes | Serves 4

680 g beef fillet, pounded to ¼	120 ml crumbled feta cheese
inch thick	60 ml finely chopped onions
3 teaspoons sea salt	2 cloves garlic, minced
1 teaspoon ground black pepper	Cooking spray
60 g creamy goat cheese	

1. Preheat the air fryer to 204°C. Spritz the air fryer basket with cooking spray. 2. Unfold the beef on a clean work surface. Rub the salt and pepper all over the beef to season. 3. Make the filling for the stuffed beef fillet: Combine the goat cheese, feta, onions, and garlic in a medium bowl. Stir until well blended. 4. Spoon the mixture in the center of the fillet. Roll the fillet up tightly like rolling a burrito and use some kitchen twine to tie the fillet. 5. Arrange the fillet in the air fryer basket and air fry for 10 minutes, flipping the fillet halfway through to ensure even cooking, or until an instant-read thermometer inserted in the center of the fillet registers 57°C for medium-rare. 6. Transfer to a platter and serve immediately.

Meat and Rice Stuffed Peppers

Prep time: 20 minutes | Cook time: 18 minutes | Serves 4

340 g lean beef mince	½ teaspoon dried basil
110 g lean pork mince	120 ml cooked brown rice
60 ml onion, minced	½ teaspoon garlic powder
1 (425 g) can finely-chopped	½ teaspoon oregano
tomatoes	½ teaspoon salt
1 teaspoon Worcestershire	2 small peppers, cut in half,
sauce	stems removed, deseeded
1 teaspoon barbecue seasoning	Cooking spray
1 teaspoon honey	

1. Preheat the air fryer to 182°C and spritz a baking pan with cooking spray. 2. Arrange the beef, pork, and onion in the baking pan and bake in the preheated air fryer for 8 minutes. Break the ground meat into chunks halfway through the cooking. 3. Meanwhile, combine the tomatoes, Worcestershire sauce, barbecue seasoning, honey, and basil in a saucepan. Stir to mix well. 4. Transfer the cooked meat mixture to a large bowl and add the cooked rice, garlic powder, oregano, salt, and 60 ml of the tomato mixture. Stir to mix well. 5. Stuff the pepper halves with the mixture, then arrange the pepper halves in the air fryer and air fry for 10 minutes or until the peppers are lightly charred. 6. Serve the stuffed peppers with the remaining tomato sauce on top.

Parmesan-Crusted Steak

Prep time: 30 minutes | Cook time: 12 minutes | Serves 6

120 ml (1 stick) unsalted butter,	almond flour
at room temperature	680 g sirloin steak
235 ml finely grated Parmesan	Sea salt and freshly ground
cheese	black pepper, to taste
60 ml finely ground blanched	

1. Place the butter, Parmesan cheese, and almond flour in a food processor. Process until smooth. Transfer to a sheet of parchment paper and form into a log. Wrap tightly in plastic wrap. Freeze for 45 minutes or refrigerate for at least 4 hours. 2. While the butter is chilling, season the steak liberally with salt and pepper. Let the steak rest at room temperature for about 45 minutes. 3. Place the grill pan or basket in your air fryer, set it to 204°C, and let it preheat for 5 minutes. 4. Working in batches, if necessary, place the steak on the grill pan and air fry for 4 minutes. Flip and cook for 3 minutes more, until the steak is brown on both sides. 5. Remove the steak from the air fryer and arrange an equal amount of the Parmesan butter on top of each steak. Return the steak to the air fryer and continue cooking for another 5 minutes, until an instant-read thermometer reads 49°C for medium-rare and the crust is golden brown (or to your desired doneness). 6. Transfer the cooked steak to a plate; let rest for 10 minutes before serving.

Fillet with Crispy Shallots

Prep time: 30 minutes | Cook time: 18 to 20 minutes | Serves 6

680 g beef fillet steaks
Sea salt and freshly ground black pepper, to taste

4 medium shallots
1 teaspoon olive oil or avocado oil

1. Season both sides of the steaks with salt and pepper, and let them sit at room temperature for 45 minutes. 2. Set the air fryer to 204ºC and let it preheat for 5 minutes. 3. Working in batches if necessary, place the steaks in the air fryer basket in a single layer and air fry for 5 minutes. Flip and cook for 5 minutes longer, until an instant-read thermometer inserted in the center of the steaks registers 49ºC for medium-rare (or as desired). Remove the steaks and tent with aluminum foil to rest. 4. Set the air fryer to 149ºC. In a medium bowl, toss the shallots with the oil. Place the shallots in the basket and air fry for 5 minutes, then give them a toss and cook for 3 to 5 minutes more, until crispy and golden brown. 5. Place the steaks on serving plates and arrange the shallots on top.

Easy Lamb Chops with Asparagus

Prep time: 10 minutes | Cook time: 15 minutes | Serves 4

4 asparagus spears, trimmed
2 tablespoons olive oil, divided
450 g lamb chops
1 garlic clove, minced

2 teaspoons chopped fresh thyme, for serving
Salt and ground black pepper, to taste

1. Preheat the air fryer to 204ºC. Spritz the air fryer basket with cooking spray. 2. On a large plate, brush the asparagus with 1 tablespoon olive oil, then sprinkle with salt. Set aside. 3. On a separate plate, brush the lamb chops with remaining olive oil and sprinkle with salt and ground black pepper. 4. Arrange the lamb chops in the preheated air fryer. Air fry for 10 minutes. 5. Flip the lamb chops and add the asparagus and garlic. Air fry for 5 more minutes or until the lamb is well browned and the asparagus is tender. 6. Serve them on a plate with thyme on top.

Greek Pork with Tzatziki Sauce

Prep time: 30 minutes | Cook time: 50 minutes | Serves 4

Greek Pork:
900 g pork loin roasting joint
Salt and black pepper, to taste
1 teaspoon smoked paprika
½ teaspoon mustard seeds
½ teaspoon celery salt
1 teaspoon fennel seeds
1 teaspoon chili powder

1 teaspoon turmeric powder
½ teaspoon ground ginger
2 tablespoons olive oil
2 cloves garlic, finely chopped
Tzatziki:
½ cucumber, finely chopped and squeezed
235 ml full-fat Greek yogurt

1 garlic clove, minced
1 tablespoon extra-virgin olive oil

1 teaspoon balsamic vinegar
1 teaspoon minced fresh dill
A pinch of salt

1. Toss all ingredients for Greek pork in a large mixing bowl. Toss until the meat is well coated. 2. Cook in the preheated air fryer at 182ºC for 30 minutes; turn over and cook another 20 minutes. 3. Meanwhile, prepare the tzatziki by mixing all the tzatziki ingredients. Place in your refrigerator until ready to use. 4. Serve the pork sirloin roast with the chilled tzatziki on the side. Enjoy!

Beef Bavette Steak with Sage

Prep time: 13 minutes | Cook time: 7 minutes | Serves 2

80 ml sour cream
120 ml spring onion, chopped
1 tablespoon mayonnaise
3 cloves garlic, smashed
450 g beef bavette or skirt steak, trimmed and cubed

2 tablespoons fresh sage, minced
½ teaspoon salt
⅓ teaspoon black pepper, or to taste

1. Season your meat with salt and pepper; arrange beef cubes on the bottom of a baking dish that fits in your air fryer. 2. Stir in spring onions and garlic; air fry for about 7 minutes at 196ºC. 3. Once your beef starts to tender, add the cream, mayonnaise, and sage; air fry an additional 8 minutes. Bon appétit!

Lemon Pork with Marjoram

Prep time: 5 minutes | Cook time: 10 minutes | Serves 4

1 (450 g) pork tenderloin, cut into ½-inch-thick slices
1 tablespoon extra-virgin olive oil
1 tablespoon freshly squeezed lemon juice
1 tablespoon honey

½ teaspoon grated lemon zest
½ teaspoon dried marjoram leaves
Pinch salt
Freshly ground black pepper, to taste
Cooking oil spray

1. Put the pork slices in a medium bowl. 2. In a small bowl, whisk the olive oil, lemon juice, honey, lemon zest, marjoram, salt, and pepper until combined. Pour this marinade over the tenderloin slices and gently massage with your hands to work it into the pork. 3. Insert the crisper plate into the basket and the basket into the unit. Preheat the unit by selecting AIR ROAST, setting the temperature to 204ºC, and setting the time to 3 minutes. Select START/STOP to begin. 4. Once the unit is preheated, spray the crisper plate with cooking oil. Place the pork into the basket. 5. Select AIR ROAST, set the temperature to 204ºC, and set the time to 10 minutes. Select START/STOP to begin. 6. When the cooking is complete, a food thermometer inserted into the pork should register at least 64ºC. Let the pork stand for 5 minutes and serve.

Pork Tenderloin with Avocado Lime Sauce

Prep time: 30 minutes | Cook time: 15 minutes | Serves 4

Marinade:
120 ml lime juice
Grated zest of 1 lime
2 teaspoons stevia glycerite, or
¼ teaspoon liquid stevia
3 cloves garlic, minced
1½ teaspoons fine sea salt
1 teaspoon chili powder, or more for more heat
1 teaspoon smoked paprika
450 g pork tenderloin
Avocado Lime Sauce:
1 medium-sized ripe avocado, roughly chopped

120 ml full-fat sour cream (or coconut cream for dairy-free)
Grated zest of 1 lime
Juice of 1 lime
2 cloves garlic, roughly chopped
½ teaspoon fine sea salt
¼ teaspoon ground black pepper
Chopped fresh coriander leaves, for garnish
Lime slices, for serving
Pico de gallo or salsa, for serving

1. In a medium-sized casserole dish, stir together all the marinade ingredients until well combined. Add the tenderloin and coat it well in the marinade. Cover and place in the fridge to marinate for 2 hours or overnight. 2. Spray the air fryer basket with avocado oil. Preheat the air fryer to 204ºC. 3. Remove the pork from the marinade and place it in the air fryer basket. Air fry for 13 to 15 minutes, until the internal temperature of the pork is 64ºC, flipping after 7 minutes. Remove the pork from the air fryer and place it on a cutting board. Allow it to rest for 8 to 10 minutes, then cut it into ½-inch-thick slices. 4. While the pork cooks, make the avocado lime sauce: Place all the sauce ingredients in a food processor and purée until smooth. Taste and adjust the seasoning to your liking. 5. Place the pork slices on a serving platter and spoon the avocado lime sauce on top. Garnish with coriander leaves and serve with lime slices and pico de gallo. 6. Store leftovers in an airtight container in the fridge for up to 4 days. Reheat in a preheated 204ºC air fryer for 5 minutes, or until heated through.

German Rouladen-Style Steak

Prep time: 20 minutes | Cook time: 15 minutes | Serves 4

Onion Sauce:
2 medium onions, cut into ½-inch-thick slices
Coarse or flaky salt and black pepper, to taste
120 ml sour cream
1 tablespoon tomato paste
2 teaspoons chopped fresh

parsley
Rouladen:
60 ml Dijon mustard
450 g bavette or skirt steak, ¼ to ½ inch thick
1 teaspoon black pepper
4 slices bacon
60 ml chopped fresh parsley

1. For the sauce: In a small bowl, mix together the onions with salt and pepper to taste. Place the onions in the air fryer basket. Set the air fryer to 204ºC for 6 minutes, or until the onions are softened and golden brown. 2. Set aside half of the onions to use in the rouladen.

Place the rest in a small bowl and add the sour cream, tomato paste, parsley, ½ teaspoon salt, and ½ teaspoon pepper. Stir until well combined, adding 1 to 2 tablespoons of water, if necessary, to thin the sauce slightly. Set the sauce aside. 3. For the rouladen: Evenly spread the mustard over the meat. Sprinkle with the pepper. Top with the bacon slices, reserved onions, and parsley. Starting at the long end, roll up the steak as tightly as possible, ending seam side down. Use 2 or 3 wooden toothpicks to hold the roll together. Using a sharp knife, cut the roll in half so that it better fits in the air fryer basket. 4. Place the steak, seam side down, in the air fryer basket. Set the air fryer to 204ºC for 9 minutes. Use a meat thermometer to ensure the steak has reached an internal temperature of 64ºC. (It is critical to not overcook bavette steak, so as to not toughen the meat.) 5. Let the steak rest for 10 minutes before cutting into slices. Serve with the sauce.

Almond and Caraway Crust Steak

Prep time: 16 minutes | Cook time: 10 minutes | Serves 4

80 ml almond flour
2 eggs
2 teaspoons caraway seeds
4 beef steaks

2 teaspoons garlic powder
1 tablespoon melted butter
Fine sea salt and cayenne pepper, to taste

1. Generously coat steaks with garlic powder, caraway seeds, salt, and cayenne pepper. 2. In a mixing dish, thoroughly combine melted butter with seasoned crumbs. In another bowl, beat the eggs until they're well whisked. 3. First, coat steaks with the beaten egg; then, coat beef steaks with the buttered crumb mixture. Place the steaks in the air fryer basket; cook for 10 minutes at 179ºC. Bon appétit!

Macadamia Nuts Crusted Pork Rack

Prep time: 5 minutes | Cook time: 35 minutes | Serves 2

1 clove garlic, minced
2 tablespoons olive oil
450 g rack of pork
235 ml chopped macadamia nuts

1 tablespoon breadcrumbs
1 tablespoon rosemary, chopped
1 egg
Salt and ground black pepper, to taste

1. Preheat the air fryer to 176ºC. 2. Combine the garlic and olive oil in a small bowl. Stir to mix well. 3. On a clean work surface, rub the pork rack with the garlic oil and sprinkle with salt and black pepper on both sides. 4. Combine the macadamia nuts, breadcrumbs, and rosemary in a shallow dish. Whisk the egg in a large bowl. 5. Dredge the pork in the egg, then roll the pork over the macadamia nut mixture to coat well. Shake the excess off. 6. Arrange the pork in the preheated air fryer and air fry for 30 minutes on both sides. Increase to 200ºC and fry for 5 more minutes or until the pork is well browned. 7. Serve immediately.

Italian Sausage and Cheese Meatballs

Prep time: 10 minutes | Cook time: 20 minutes | Serves 4

230 g sausage meat with Italian seasoning added to taste
230 g 85% lean beef mince
120 ml shredded sharp Cheddar

cheese
½ teaspoon onion granules
½ teaspoon garlic powder
½ teaspoon black pepper

1. In a large bowl, gently mix the sausage meat, beef mince, cheese, onion granules, garlic powder, and pepper until well combined. 2. Form the mixture into 16 meatballs. Place the meatballs in a single layer in the air fryer basket. Set the air fryer to 176°C for 20 minutes, turning the meatballs halfway through the cooking time. Use a meat thermometer to ensure the meatballs have reached an internal temperature of 72°C (medium).

Herbed Beef

Prep time: 5 minutes | Cook time: 22 minutes | Serves 6

1 teaspoon dried dill
1 teaspoon dried thyme
1 teaspoon garlic powder

900 g beef steak
3 tablespoons butter

1. Preheat the air fryer to 182°C. 2. Combine the dill, thyme, and garlic powder in a small bowl, and massage into the steak. 3. Air fry the steak in the air fryer for 20 minutes, then remove, shred, and return to the air fryer. 4. Add the butter and air fry the shredded steak for a further 2 minutes at 185°C. Make sure the beef is coated in the butter before serving.

Lemony Pork Loin Chop Schnitzel

Prep time: 15 minutes | Cook time: 15 minutes | Serves 4

4 thin boneless pork loin chops
2 tablespoons lemon juice
120 ml flour
¼ teaspoon marjoram
1 teaspoon salt

235 ml panko breadcrumbs
2 eggs
Lemon wedges, for serving
Cooking spray

1. Preheat the air fryer to 200°C and spritz with cooking spray. 2. On a clean work surface, drizzle the pork chops with lemon juice on both sides. 3. Combine the flour with marjoram and salt on a shallow plate. Pour the breadcrumbs on a separate shallow dish. Beat the eggs in a large bowl. 4. Dredge the pork chops in the flour, then dunk in the beaten eggs to coat well. Shake the excess off and roll over the breadcrumbs. 5. Arrange the chops in the preheated air fryer and spritz with cooking spray. Air fry for 15 minutes or until the chops are golden and crispy. Flip the chops halfway through. Squeeze the lemon wedges over the fried chops and serve immediately.

Caraway Crusted Beef Steaks

Prep time: 5 minutes | Cook time: 10 minutes | Serves 4

4 beef steaks
2 teaspoons caraway seeds
2 teaspoons garlic powder
Sea salt and cayenne pepper, to

taste
1 tablespoon melted butter
80 ml almond flour
2 eggs, beaten

1. Preheat the air fryer to 179°C. 2. Add the beef steaks to a large bowl and toss with the caraway seeds, garlic powder, salt and pepper until well coated. 3. Stir together the melted butter and almond flour in a bowl. Whisk the eggs in a different bowl. 4. Dredge the seasoned steaks in the eggs, then dip in the almond and butter mixture. 5. Arrange the coated steaks in the air fryer basket. Air fryer for 10 minutes, or until the internal temperature of the beef steaks reaches at least 64°C on a meat thermometer. Flip the steaks once halfway through to ensure even cooking. 6. Transfer the steaks to plates. Let cool for 5 minutes and serve hot.

Bo Luc Lac

Prep time: 50 minutes | Cook time: 8 minutes | Serves 4

For the Meat:
2 teaspoons soy sauce
4 garlic cloves, minced
1 teaspoon coarse or flaky salt
2 teaspoons sugar
¼ teaspoon ground black pepper
1 teaspoon toasted sesame oil
680 g top rump steak, cut into 1-inch cubes
Cooking spray
For the Salad:
1 head butterhead lettuce, leaves separated and torn into large pieces
60 ml fresh mint leaves

120 ml halved baby plum tomatoes
½ red onion, halved and thinly sliced
2 tablespoons apple cider vinegar
1 garlic clove, minced
2 teaspoons sugar
¼ teaspoon coarse or flaky salt
¼ teaspoon ground black pepper
2 tablespoons vegetable oil
For Serving:
Lime wedges, for garnish
Coarse salt and freshly cracked black pepper, to taste

1. Combine the ingredients for the meat, except for the steak, in a large bowl. Stir to mix well. 2. Dunk the steak cubes in the bowl and press to coat. Wrap the bowl in plastic and marinate under room temperature for at least 30 minutes. 3. Preheat the air fryer to 232°C. Spritz the air fryer basket with cooking spray. 4. Discard the marinade and transfer the steak cubes in the preheated air fryer basket. You need to air fry in batches to avoid overcrowding. 5. Air fry for 4 minutes or until the steak cubes are lightly browned but still have a little pink. Shake the basket halfway through the cooking time. 6. Meanwhile, combine the ingredients for the salad in a separate large bowl. Toss to mix well. 7. Pour the salad in a large serving bowl and top with the steak cubes. Squeeze the lime wedges over and sprinkle with salt and black pepper before serving.

Sausage and Pork Meatballs

Prep time: 15 minutes | Cook time: 8 to 12 minutes | Serves 8

1 large egg
1 teaspoon gelatin
450 g pork mince
230 g Italian-seasoned sausage, casings removed, crumbled
80 ml Parmesan cheese
60 ml finely diced onion
1 tablespoon tomato paste
1 teaspoon minced garlic
1 teaspoon dried oregano
¼ teaspoon red pepper flakes
Sea salt and freshly ground black pepper, to taste
Keto-friendly marinara sauce, for serving

1. Beat the egg in a small bowl and sprinkle with the gelatin. Allow to sit for 5 minutes. 2. In a large bowl, combine the pork mince, sausage, Parmesan, onion, tomato paste, garlic, oregano, and red pepper flakes. Season with salt and black pepper. 3. Stir the gelatin mixture, then add it to the other ingredients and, using clean hands, mix to ensure that everything is well combined. Form into 1½-inch round meatballs. 4. Set the air fryer to 204ºC. Place the meatballs in the air fryer basket in a single layer, cooking in batches as needed. Air fry for 5 minutes. Flip and cook for 3 to 7 minutes more, or until an instant-read thermometer reads 72ºC.

Greek Stuffed Fillet

Prep time: 10 minutes | Cook time: 10 minutes | Serves 4

680 g venison or beef fillet, pounded to ¼ inch thick
3 teaspoons fine sea salt
1 teaspoon ground black pepper
60 g creamy goat cheese
120 ml crumbled feta cheese (about 60 g)
60 ml finely chopped onions
2 cloves garlic, minced
For Garnish/Serving (Optional):
Yellow/American mustard
Halved cherry tomatoes
Extra-virgin olive oil
Sprigs of fresh rosemary
Lavender flowers

1. Spray the air fryer basket with avocado oil. Preheat the air fryer to 204ºC. 2. Season the fillet on all sides with the salt and pepper. 3. In a medium-sized mixing bowl, combine the goat cheese, feta, onions, and garlic. Place the mixture in the center of the tenderloin. Starting at the end closest to you, tightly roll the tenderloin like a jelly roll. Tie the rolled tenderloin tightly with kitchen twine. 4. Place the meat in the air fryer basket and air fry for 5 minutes. Flip the meat over and cook for another 5 minutes, or until the internal temperature reaches 57ºC for medium-rare. 5. To serve, smear a line of yellow mustard on a platter, then place the meat next to it and add halved cherry tomatoes on the side, if desired. Drizzle with olive oil and garnish with rosemary sprigs and lavender flowers, if desired. 6. Best served fresh. Store leftovers in an airtight container in the fridge for 3 days. Reheat in a preheated 176ºC air fryer for 4 minutes, or until heated through.

Crescent Dogs

Prep time: 15 minutes | Cook time: 8 minutes | Makes 24 crescent dogs

Oil, for spraying
1 (230 g) can ready-to-bake croissants
8 slices Cheddar cheese, cut into thirds
24 cocktail sausages or 8 (6-inch) hot dogs, cut into thirds
2 tablespoons unsalted butter, melted
1 tablespoon sea salt flakes

1. Line the air fryer basket with parchment and spray lightly with oil. 2. Separate the dough into 8 triangles. Cut each triangle into 3 narrow triangles so you have 24 total triangles. 3. Top each triangle with 1 piece of cheese and 1 cocktail sausage. 4. Roll up each piece of dough, starting at the wide end and rolling toward the point. 5. Place the rolls in the prepared basket in a single layer. You may need to cook in batches, depending on the size of your air fryer. 6. Air fry at 164ºC for 3 to 4 minutes, flip, and cook for another 3 to 4 minutes, or until golden brown. 7. Brush with the melted butter and sprinkle with the sea salt flakes before serving.

Kheema Burgers

Prep time: 15 minutes | Cook time: 12 minutes | Serves 4

Burgers:
450 g 85% lean beef mince or lamb mince
2 large eggs, lightly beaten
1 medium brown onion, diced
60 ml chopped fresh coriander
1 tablespoon minced fresh ginger
3 cloves garlic, minced
2 teaspoons garam masala
1 teaspoon ground turmeric
½ teaspoon ground cinnamon
⅛ teaspoon ground cardamom
1 teaspoon coarse or flaky salt
1 teaspoon cayenne pepper
Raita Sauce:
235 ml grated cucumber
120 ml sour cream
¼ teaspoon coarse or flaky salt
¼ teaspoon black pepper
For Serving:
4 lettuce leaves, hamburger buns, or naan breads

1. For the burgers: In a large bowl, combine the beef mince, eggs, onion, coriander, ginger, garlic, garam masala, turmeric, cinnamon, cardamom, salt, and cayenne. Gently mix until ingredients are thoroughly combined. 2. Divide the meat into four portions and form into round patties. Make a slight depression in the middle of each patty with your thumb to prevent them from puffing up into a dome shape while cooking. 3. Place the patties in the air fryer basket. Set the air fryer to 176ºC for 12 minutes. Use a meat thermometer to ensure the burgers have reached an internal temperature of 72ºC (for medium). 4. Meanwhile, for the sauce: In a small bowl, combine the cucumber, sour cream, salt, and pepper. 5. To serve: Place the burgers on the lettuce, buns, or naan and top with the sauce.

Short Ribs with Chimichurri

Prep time: 30 minutes | Cook time: 13 minutes | Serves 4

450 g boneless short ribs	1 tablespoon freshly squeezed
1½ teaspoons sea salt, divided	lemon juice
½ teaspoon freshly ground	½ teaspoon ground cumin
black pepper, divided	¼ teaspoon red pepper flakes
120 ml fresh parsley leaves	2 tablespoons extra-virgin olive
120 ml fresh coriander leaves	oil
1 teaspoon minced garlic	Avocado oil spray

1. Pat the short ribs dry with paper towels. Sprinkle the ribs all over with 1 teaspoon salt and ¼ teaspoon black pepper. Let sit at room temperature for 45 minutes. 2. Meanwhile, place the parsley, coriander, garlic, lemon juice, cumin, red pepper flakes, the remaining ½ teaspoon salt, and the remaining ¼ teaspoon black pepper in a blender or food processor. With the blender running, slowly drizzle in the olive oil. Blend for about 1 minute, until the mixture is smooth and well combined. 3. Set the air fryer to 204ºC. Spray both sides of the ribs with oil. Place in the basket and air fry for 8 minutes. Flip and cook for another 5 minutes, until an instant-read thermometer reads 52ºC for medium-rare (or to your desired doneness). 4. Allow the meat to rest for 5 to 10 minutes, then slice. Serve warm with the chimichurri sauce.

Herb-Roasted Beef Tips with Onions

Prep time: 5 minutes | Cook time: 10 minutes | Serves 4

450 g rib eye steak, cubed	1 teaspoon salt
2 garlic cloves, minced	½ teaspoon black pepper
2 tablespoons olive oil	1 brown onion, thinly sliced
1 tablespoon fresh oregano	

1. Preheat the air fryer to 192ºC. 2. In a medium bowl, combine the steak, garlic, olive oil, oregano, salt, pepper, and onion. Mix until all of the beef and onion are well coated. 3. Put the seasoned steak mixture into the air fryer basket. Roast for 5 minutes. Stir and roast for 5 minutes more. 4. Let rest for 5 minutes before serving with some favorite sides.

Rosemary Roast Beef

Prep time: 30 minutes | Cook time: 30 to 35 minutes | Serves 8

1 (900 g) beef roasting joint,	2 teaspoons minced garlic
tied with kitchen string	2 tablespoons finely chopped
Sea salt and freshly ground	fresh rosemary
black pepper, to taste	60 ml avocado oil

1. Season the roast generously with salt and pepper. 2. In a small bowl, whisk together the garlic, rosemary, and avocado oil. Rub this all over the roast. Cover loosely with aluminum foil or plastic wrap and refrigerate for at least 12 hours or up to 2 days. 3. Remove the roast from the refrigerator and allow to sit at room temperature for about 1 hour. 4. Set the air fryer to 164ºC. Place the roast in the air fryer basket and roast for 15 minutes. Flip the roast and cook for 15 to 20 minutes more, until the meat is browned and an instant-read thermometer reads 49ºC at the thickest part (for medium-rare). 5. Transfer the meat to a cutting board, and let it rest for 15 minutes before thinly slicing and serving.

Spicy Lamb Sirloin Chops

Prep time: 30 minutes | Cook time: 15 minutes | Serves 4

½ brown onion, coarsely	1 teaspoon ground cinnamon
chopped	1 teaspoon ground turmeric
4 coin-size slices peeled fresh	½ to 1 teaspoon cayenne pepper
ginger	½ teaspoon ground cardamom
5 garlic cloves	1 teaspoon coarse or flaky salt
1 teaspoon garam masala	450 g lamb sirloin chops
1 teaspoon ground fennel	

1. In a blender, combine the onion, ginger, garlic, garam masala, fennel, cinnamon, turmeric, cayenne, cardamom, and salt. Pulse until the onion is finely minced and the mixture forms a thick paste, 3 to 4 minutes. 2. Place the lamb chops in a large bowl. Slash the meat and fat with a sharp knife several times to allow the marinade to penetrate better. Add the spice paste to the bowl and toss the lamb to coat. Marinate at room temperature for 30 minutes or cover and refrigerate for up to 24 hours. 3. Place the lamb chops in a single layer in the air fryer basket. Set the air fryer to 164ºC for 15 minutes, turning the chops halfway through the cooking time. Use a meat thermometer to ensure the lamb has reached an internal temperature of 64ºC (medium-rare).

Italian Lamb Chops with Avocado Mayo

Prep time: 5 minutes | Cook time: 12 minutes | Serves 2

2 lamp chops	120 ml mayonnaise
2 teaspoons Italian herbs	1 tablespoon lemon juice
2 avocados	

1. Season the lamb chops with the Italian herbs, then set aside for 5 minutes. 2. Preheat the air fryer to 204ºC and place the rack inside. 3. Put the chops on the rack and air fry for 12 minutes. 4. In the meantime, halve the avocados and open to remove the pits. Spoon the flesh into a blender. 5. Add the mayonnaise and lemon juice and pulse until a smooth consistency is achieved. 6. Take care when removing the chops from the air fryer, then plate up and serve with the avocado mayo.

Lebanese Malfouf (Stuffed Cabbage Rolls)

Prep time: 15 minutes | Cook time: 33 minutes | Serves 4

1 head green cabbage	2 tablespoons chopped fresh
450 g lean beef mince	mint
120 ml long-grain brown rice	Juice of 1 lemon
4 garlic cloves, minced	Olive oil cooking spray
1 teaspoon salt	120 ml beef stock
½ teaspoon black pepper	1 tablespoon olive oil
1 teaspoon ground cinnamon	

1. Cut the cabbage in half and remove the core. Remove 12 of the larger leaves to use for the cabbage rolls. 2. Bring a large pot of salted water to a boil, then drop the cabbage leaves into the water, boiling them for 3 minutes. Remove from the water and set aside. 3. In a large bowl, combine the beef, rice, garlic, salt, pepper, cinnamon, mint, and lemon juice, and mix together until combined. Divide this mixture into 12 equal portions. 4. Preheat the air fryer to 182ºC. Lightly coat a small casserole dish with olive oil cooking spray. 5. Place a cabbage leaf on a clean work surface. Place a spoonful of the beef mixture on one side of the leaf, leaving space on all other sides. Fold the two perpendicular sides inward and then roll forward, tucking tightly as rolled (similar to a burrito roll). Place the finished rolls into the baking dish, stacking them on top of each other if needed. 6. Pour the beef stock over the top of the cabbage rolls so that it soaks down between them, and then brush the tops with the olive oil. 7. Place the casserole dish into the air fryer basket and bake for 30 minutes.

Bacon-Wrapped Hot Dogs with Mayo-Ketchup Sauce

Prep time: 5 minutes | Cook time: 10 to 12 minutes | Serves 5

10 thin slices of bacon	60 ml mayonnaise
5 pork hot dogs, halved	4 tablespoons ketchup
1 teaspoon cayenne pepper	1 teaspoon rice vinegar
Sauce:	1 teaspoon chili powder

1. Preheat the air fryer to 200ºC. 2. Arrange the slices of bacon on a clean work surface. One by one, place the halved hot dog on one end of each slice, season with cayenne pepper and wrap the hot dog with the bacon slices and secure with toothpicks as needed. 3. Work in batches, place half the wrapped hot dogs in the air fryer basket and air fry for 10 to 12 minutes or until the bacon becomes browned and crispy. 4. Make the sauce: Stir all the ingredients for the sauce in a small bowl. Wrap the bowl in plastic and set in the refrigerator until ready to serve. 5. Transfer the hot dogs to a platter and serve hot with the sauce.

Steak with Bell Pepper

Prep time: 30 minutes | Cook time: 20 to 23 minutes | Serves 6

60 ml avocado oil	450 g top rump steak or bavette
60 ml freshly squeezed lime	or skirt steak, thinly sliced
juice	against the grain
2 teaspoons minced garlic	1 red pepper, cored, seeded, and
1 tablespoon chili powder	cut into ½-inch slices
½ teaspoon ground cumin	1 green pepper, cored, seeded,
Sea salt and freshly ground	and cut into ½-inch slices
black pepper, to taste	1 large onion, sliced

1. In a small bowl or blender, combine the avocado oil, lime juice, garlic, chili powder, cumin, and salt and pepper to taste. 2. Place the sliced steak in a zip-top bag or shallow dish. Place the peppers and onion in a separate zip-top bag or dish. Pour half the marinade over the steak and the other half over the vegetables. Seal both bags and let the steak and vegetables marinate in the refrigerator for at least 1 hour or up to 4 hours. 3. Line the air fryer basket with an air fryer liner or aluminum foil. Remove the vegetables from their bag or dish and shake off any excess marinade. Set the air fryer to 204ºC. Place the vegetables in the air fryer basket and cook for 13 minutes. 4. Remove the steak from its bag or dish and shake off any excess marinade. Place the steak on top of the vegetables in the air fryer, and cook for 7 to 10 minutes or until an instant-read thermometer reads 49ºC for medium-rare (or cook to your desired doneness). 5. Serve with desired fixings, such as keto tortillas, lettuce, sour cream, avocado slices, shredded Cheddar cheese, and coriander.

Super Bacon with Meat

Prep time: 5 minutes | Cook time: 1 hour | Serves 4

30 slices thick-cut bacon	280 g pork sausage meat
110 g Cheddar cheese, shredded	Salt and ground black pepper,
340 g steak	to taste

1. Preheat the air fryer to 204ºC. 2. Lay out 30 slices of bacon in a woven pattern and bake for 20 minutes until crisp. Put the cheese in the center of the bacon. 3. Combine the steak and sausage to form a meaty mixture. 4. Lay out the meat in a rectangle of similar size to the bacon strips. Season with salt and pepper. 5. Roll the meat into a tight roll and refrigerate. 6. Preheat the air fryer to 204ºC. 7. Make a 7×7 bacon weave and roll the bacon weave over the meat, diagonally. 8. Bake for 60 minutes or until the internal temperature reaches at least 74ºC. 9. Let rest for 5 minutes before serving.

Mozzarella Stuffed Beef and Pork Meatballs

Prep time: 15 minutes | Cook time: 12 minutes |
Serves 4 to 6

1 tablespoon olive oil	½ teaspoon dried oregano
1 small onion, finely chopped	1½ teaspoons salt
1 to 2 cloves garlic, minced	Freshly ground black pepper, to
340 g beef mince	taste
340 g pork mince	2 eggs, lightly beaten
180 ml bread crumbs	140 g low-moisture Mozzarella
60 ml grated Parmesan cheese	or other melting cheese, cut into
60 ml finely chopped fresh	1-inch cubes
parsley	

1. Preheat a skillet over medium-high heat. Add the oil and cook the onion and garlic until tender, but not browned. 2. Transfer the onion and garlic to a large bowl and add the beef, pork, bread crumbs, Parmesan cheese, parsley, oregano, salt, pepper and eggs. Mix well until all the ingredients are combined. Divide the mixture into 12 evenly sized balls. Make one meatball at a time, by pressing a hole in the meatball mixture with the finger and pushing a piece of Mozzarella cheese into the hole. Mold the meat back into a ball, enclosing the cheese. 3. Preheat the air fryer to 192°C. 4. Working in two batches, transfer six of the meatballs to the air fryer basket and air fry for 12 minutes, shaking the basket and turning the meatballs twice during the cooking process. Repeat with the remaining 6 meatballs. Serve warm.

Beef Mince Taco Rolls

Prep time: 20 minutes | Cook time: 10 minutes | Serves 4

230 g 80/20 beef mince	coriander
80 ml water	355 ml shredded Mozzarella
1 tablespoon chili powder	cheese
2 teaspoons cumin	120 ml blanched finely ground
½ teaspoon garlic powder	almond flour
¼ teaspoon dried oregano	60 g full-fat cream cheese
60 ml tinned diced tomatoes	1 large egg
2 tablespoons chopped	

1. In a medium skillet over medium heat, brown the beef mince about 7 to 10 minutes. When meat is fully cooked, drain. 2. Add water to skillet and stir in chili powder, cumin, garlic powder, oregano, and tomatoes. Add coriander. Bring to a boil, then reduce heat to simmer for 3 minutes. 3. In a large microwave-safe bowl, place Mozzarella, almond flour, cream cheese, and egg. Microwave for 1 minute. Stir the mixture quickly until smooth ball of dough forms. 4. Cut a piece of parchment for your work surface. Press the dough into a large rectangle on the parchment, wetting your hands to prevent the dough from sticking as necessary. Cut the dough into eight rectangles. 5. On each rectangle place a few spoons of the

meat mixture. Fold the short ends of each roll toward the center and roll the length as you would a burrito. 6. Cut a piece of parchment to fit your air fryer basket. Place taco rolls onto the parchment and place into the air fryer basket. 7. Adjust the temperature to 182°C and air fry for 10 minutes. 8. Flip halfway through the cooking time. 9. Allow to cool 10 minutes before serving.

Steaks with Walnut-Blue Cheese Butter

Prep time: 30 minutes | Cook time: 10 minutes | Serves 6

120 ml unsalted butter, at room	1 teaspoon minced garlic
temperature	¼ teaspoon cayenne pepper
120 ml crumbled blue cheese	Sea salt and freshly ground
2 tablespoons finely chopped	black pepper, to taste
walnuts	680 g sirloin steaks, at room
1 tablespoon minced fresh	temperature
rosemary	

1. In a medium bowl, combine the butter, blue cheese, walnuts, rosemary, garlic, and cayenne pepper and salt and black pepper to taste. Use clean hands to ensure that everything is well combined. Place the mixture on a sheet of parchment paper and form it into a log. Wrap it tightly in plastic wrap. Refrigerate for at least 2 hours or freeze for 30 minutes. 2. Season the steaks generously with salt and pepper. 3. Place the air fryer basket or grill pan in the air fryer. Set the air fryer to 204°C and let it preheat for 5 minutes. 4. Place the steaks in the basket in a single layer and air fry for 5 minutes. Flip the steaks, and cook for 5 minutes more, until an instant-read thermometer reads 49°C for medium-rare (or as desired). 5. Transfer the steaks to a plate. Cut the butter into pieces and place the desired amount on top of the steaks. Tent a piece of aluminum foil over the steaks and allow to sit for 10 minutes before serving. 6. Store any remaining butter in a sealed container in the refrigerator for up to 2 weeks.

Mexican Pork Chops

Prep time: 5 minutes | Cook time: 15 minutes | Serves 2

¼ teaspoon dried oregano	2 (110 g) boneless pork chops
1½ teaspoons taco seasoning or	2 tablespoons unsalted butter,
fajita seasoning mix	divided

1. Preheat the air fryer to 204°C. 2. Combine the dried oregano and taco seasoning in a small bowl and rub the mixture into the pork chops. Brush the chops with 1 tablespoon butter. 3. In the air fryer, air fry the chops for 15 minutes, turning them over halfway through to air fry on the other side. 4. When the chops are a brown color, check the internal temperature has reached 64°C and remove from the air fryer. Serve with a garnish of remaining butter.

Kheema Meatloaf

450 g 85% lean beef mince

2 large eggs, lightly beaten

235 ml diced brown onion

60 ml chopped fresh coriander

1 tablespoon minced fresh ginger

1 tablespoon minced garlic

2 teaspoons garam masala

1 teaspoon coarse or flaky salt

1 teaspoon ground turmeric

1 teaspoon cayenne pepper

½ teaspoon ground cinnamon

⅛ teaspoon ground cardamom

1. In a large bowl, gently mix the beef mince, eggs, onion, coriander, ginger, garlic, garam masala, salt, turmeric, cayenne, cinnamon, and cardamom until thoroughly combined. 2. Place the seasoned meat in a baking pan. Place the pan in the air fryer basket. Set the air fryer to 176°C for 15 minutes. Use a meat thermometer to ensure the meat loaf has reached an internal temperature of 72°C (medium). 3. Drain the fat and liquid from the pan and let stand for 5 minutes before slicing. 4. Slice and serve hot.

Beef and Spinach Rolls

3 teaspoons pesto

900 g beef bavette or skirt steak

6 slices low-moisture Mozarella or other melting cheese

85 g roasted red peppers

180 ml baby spinach

1 teaspoon sea salt

1 teaspoon black pepper

1. Preheat the air fryer to 204°C. 2. Spoon equal amounts of the pesto onto each steak and spread it across evenly. 3. Put the cheese, roasted red peppers and spinach on top of the meat, about three-quarters of the way down. 4. Roll the steak up, holding it in place with toothpicks. Sprinkle with the sea salt and pepper. 5. Put inside the air fryer and air fry for 14 minutes, turning halfway through the cooking time. 6. Allow the beef to rest for 10 minutes before slicing up and serving.

Chapter 7 Fish and Seafood

Parmesan Fish Fillets

Prep time: 8 minutes | Cook time: 17 minutes | Serves 4

50 g grated Parmesan cheese
½ teaspoon fennel seed
½ teaspoon tarragon
⅓ teaspoon mixed peppercorns

2 eggs, beaten
4 (110 g) fish fillets, halved
2 tablespoons dry white wine
1 teaspoon seasoned salt

1. Preheat the air fryer to 174ºC. 2. Place the grated Parmesan cheese, fennel seed, tarragon, and mixed peppercorns in a food processor and pulse for about 20 seconds until well combined. Transfer the cheese mixture to a shallow dish. 3. Place the beaten eggs in another shallow dish. 4. Drizzle the dry white wine over the top of fish fillets. Dredge each fillet in the beaten eggs on both sides, shaking off any excess, then roll them in the cheese mixture until fully coated. Season with the salt. 5. Arrange the fillets in the air fryer basket and air fry for about 17 minutes, or until the fish is cooked through and no longer translucent. Flip the fillets once halfway through the cooking time. 6. Cool for 5 minutes before serving.

Salmon with Provolone Cheese

Prep time: 5 minutes | Cook time: 15 minutes | Serves 4

455 g salmon fillet, chopped
60 g Provolone or Edam, grated

1 teaspoon avocado oil
¼ teaspoon ground paprika

1. Sprinkle the salmon fillets with avocado oil and put in the air fryer. 2. Then sprinkle the fish with ground paprika and top with Provolone cheese. 3. Cook the fish at 182ºC for 15 minutes.

Tandoori Prawns

Prep time: 25 minutes | Cook time: 6 minutes | Serves 4

455 g jumbo raw prawns (21 to 25 count), peeled and deveined
1 tablespoon minced fresh ginger
3 cloves garlic, minced
5 g chopped fresh coriander or parsley, plus more for garnish

1 teaspoon ground turmeric
1 teaspoon garam masala
1 teaspoon smoked paprika
1 teaspoon kosher or coarse sea salt
½ to 1 teaspoon cayenne pepper
2 tablespoons olive oil (for

Paleo) or melted ghee

2 teaspoons fresh lemon juice

1. In a large bowl, combine the prawns, ginger, garlic, coriander, turmeric, garam masala, paprika, salt, and cayenne. Toss well to coat. Add the oil or ghee and toss again. Marinate at room temperature for 15 minutes, or cover and refrigerate for up to 8 hours. 2. Place the prawns in a single layer in the air fryer basket. Set the air fryer to 164ºC for 6 minutes. Transfer the prawns to a serving platter. Cover and let the prawns finish cooking in the residual heat, about 5 minutes. 3. Sprinkle the prawns with the lemon juice and toss to coat. Garnish with additional cilantro and serve.

Paprika Prawns

Prep time: 5 minutes | Cook time: 6 minutes | Serves 2

230 g medium prawns, peeled and deveined
2 tablespoons salted butter, melted

1 teaspoon paprika
½ teaspoon garlic powder
¼ teaspoon onion powder
½ teaspoon Old Bay seasoning

1. Toss all ingredients together in a large bowl. Place prawns into the air fryer basket. 2. Adjust the temperature to 204ºC and set the timer for 6 minutes. 3. Turn the prawns halfway through the cooking time to ensure even cooking. Serve immediately.

Greek Fish Pitas

Prep time: 10 minutes | Cook time: 15 minutes | Serves 4

455 g pollock, cut into 1-inch pieces
60 ml olive oil
1 teaspoon salt
½ teaspoon dried oregano
½ teaspoon dried thyme
½ teaspoon garlic powder

¼ teaspoon cayenne
4 whole wheat pitas
75 g shredded lettuce
2 plum tomatoes, diced
Nonfat plain Greek yogurt
Lemon, quartered

1. Preheat the air fryer to 192ºC. 2. In a medium bowl, combine the pollock with olive oil, salt, oregano, thyme, garlic powder, and cayenne. 3. Put the pollock into the air fryer basket and roast for 15 minutes. 4. Serve inside pitas with lettuce, tomato, and Greek yogurt with a lemon wedge on the side.

Baked Grouper with Tomatoes and Garlic

Prep time: 5 minutes | Cook time: 12 minutes | Serves 4

4 grouper fillets
½ teaspoon salt
3 garlic cloves, minced
1 tomato, sliced

45 g sliced Kalamata olives
10 g fresh dill, roughly chopped
Juice of 1 lemon
¼ cup olive oil

1. Preheat the air fryer to 192ºC. 2. Season the grouper fillets on all sides with salt, then place into the air fryer basket and top with the minced garlic, tomato slices, olives, and fresh dill. 3. Drizzle the lemon juice and olive oil over the top of the grouper, then bake for 10 to 12 minutes, or until the internal temperature reaches 64ºC.

Salmon with Fennel and Carrot

Prep time: 15 minutes | Cook time: 15 minutes | Serves 4

1 fennel bulb, thinly sliced
2 large carrots, sliced
1 large onion, thinly sliced
2 teaspoons extra-virgin olive oil
120 ml sour cream

1 teaspoon dried tarragon leaves
4 (140 g) salmon fillets
⅛ teaspoon salt
¼ teaspoon coarsely ground black pepper

1. Insert the crisper plate into the basket and the basket into the unit. Preheat the unit to204ºC, 2. In a medium bowl, toss together the fennel, carrots, and onion. Add the olive oil and toss again to coat the vegetables. Put the vegetables into a 6-inch round metal pan. 3. Once the unit is preheated, place the pan into the basket. 4. Cook for 15 minutes. 5. Check after 5 minutes, the vegetables should be crisp-tender. Remove the pan and stir in the sour cream and tarragon. Top with the salmon fillets and sprinkle the fish with the salt and pepper. Reinsert the pan into the basket and resume cooking. 6. When the cooking is complete, the salmon should flake easily with a fork and a food thermometer should register at least 64ºC. Serve the salmon on top of the vegetables.

Simple Buttery Cod

Prep time: 5 minutes | Cook time: 8 minutes | Serves 2

2 cod fillets, 110 g each
2 tablespoons salted butter, melted

1 teaspoon Old Bay seasoning
½ medium lemon, sliced

1. Place cod fillets into a round baking dish. Brush each fillet with butter and sprinkle with Old Bay seasoning. Lay two lemon slices on each fillet. Cover the dish with foil and place into the air fryer basket. 2. Adjust the temperature to 176ºC and bake for 8 minutes. Flip halfway through the cooking time. When cooked, internal temperature should be at least 64ºC. Serve warm.

Tuna Avocado Bites

Prep time: 10 minutes | Cook time: 7 minutes | Makes 12 bites

280 g can tuna, drained
60 ml full-fat mayonnaise
1 stalk celery, chopped
1 medium avocado, peeled,

pitted, and mashed
50 g blanched finely ground almond flour, divided
2 teaspoons coconut oil

1. In a large bowl, mix tuna, mayonnaise, celery, and mashed avocado. Form the mixture into balls. 2. Roll balls in almond flour and spritz with coconut oil. Place balls into the air fryer basket. 3. Adjust the temperature to 204ºC and set the timer for 7 minutes. 4. Gently turn tuna bites after 5 minutes. Serve warm.

Almond-Crusted Fish

Prep time: 15 minutes | Cook time: 10 minutes | Serves 4

4 firm white fish fillets, 110g each
45 g breadcrumbs
20 g slivered almonds, crushed
2 tablespoons lemon juice
⅛ teaspoon cayenne

Salt and pepper, to taste
940 g plain flour
1 egg, beaten with 1 tablespoon water
Olive or vegetable oil for misting or cooking spray

1. Split fish fillets lengthwise down the center to create 8 pieces. 2. Mix breadcrumbs and almonds together and set aside. 3. Mix the lemon juice and cayenne together. Brush on all sides of fish. 4. Season fish to taste with salt and pepper. 5. Place the flour on a sheet of wax paper. 6. Roll fillets in flour, dip in egg wash, and roll in the crumb mixture. 7. Mist both sides of fish with oil or cooking spray. 8. Spray the air fryer basket and lay fillets inside. 9. Roast at 200ºC for 5 minutes, turn fish over, and cook for an additional 5 minutes or until fish is done and flakes easily.

Air Fryer Fish Fry

Prep time: 5 minutes | Cook time: 15 minutes | Serves 4

470 ml low-fat buttermilk
½ teaspoon garlic powder
½ teaspoon onion powder
4 (110 g) sole fillets

70 g plain yellow cornmeal
45 g chickpea flour
¼ teaspoon cayenne pepper
Freshly ground black pepper

1. In a large bowl, combine the buttermilk, garlic powder, and onion powder. 2. Add the sole, turning until well coated, and set aside to marinate for 20 minutes. 3. In a shallow bowl, stir the cornmeal, chickpea flour, cayenne, and pepper together. 4. Dredge the fillets in the meal mixture, turning until well coated. Place in the basket of an air fryer. 5. Set the air fryer to 192ºC, close, and cook for 12 minutes.

Cayenne Sole Cutlets

Prep time: 15 minutes | Cook time: 10 minutes | Serves 2

1 egg	taste
120 g Pecorino Romano cheese, grated	½ teaspoon cayenne pepper
	1 teaspoon dried parsley flakes
Sea salt and white pepper, to	2 sole fillets

1. To make a breading station, whisk the egg until frothy. 2. In another bowl, mix Pecorino Romano cheese, and spices. 3. Dip the fish in the egg mixture and turn to coat evenly; then, dredge in the cracker crumb mixture, turning a couple of times to coat evenly. 4. Cook in the preheated air fryer at 200ºC for 5 minutes; turn them over and cook another 5 minutes. Enjoy!

Cod with Jalapeño

Prep time: 5 minutes | Cook time: 14 minutes | Serves 4

4 cod fillets, boneless	1 tablespoon avocado oil
1 jalapeño, minced	½ teaspoon minced garlic

1. In the shallow bowl, mix minced jalapeño, avocado oil, and minced garlic. 2. Put the cod fillets in the air fryer basket in one layer and top with minced jalapeño mixture. 3. Cook the fish at 185ºC for 7 minutes per side.

Jalea

Prep time: 20 minutes | Cook time: 10 minutes | Serves 4

Salsa Criolla☐	20 large or jumbo prawns, peeled and deveined
½ red onion, thinly sliced	
2 tomatoes, diced	30 g plain flour
1 serrano or jalapeño pepper, deseeded and diced	40 g cornflour
	1 teaspoon garlic powder
1 clove garlic, minced	1 teaspoon kosher or coarse sea salt
5 g chopped fresh coriander	
Pinch of kosher or coarse sea salt	¼ teaspoon cayenne pepper
	240 g panko bread crumbs
3 limes	2 eggs, beaten with 2 tablespoons water
Fried Seafood☐	
455 g firm, white-fleshed fish such as cod (add an extra 230 g fish if not using prawns)	Vegetable oil, for spraying
	Mayonnaise or tartar sauce, for serving (optional)

1. To make the Salsa Criolla, combine the red onion, tomatoes, pepper, garlic, cilantro, and salt in a medium bowl. Add the juice and zest of 2 of the limes. Refrigerate the salad while you make the fish. 2. To make the seafood, cut the fish fillets into strips approximately 2 inches long and 1 inch wide. Place the flour, cornstarch, garlic powder, salt, and cayenne pepper on a plate and whisk to combine. Place the panko on a separate plate. Dredge the fish strips in the seasoned flour mixture, shaking off any excess. Dip the strips in the egg mixture, coating them completely, then dredge in the panko, shaking off any excess. Place the fish strips on a plate or rack. Repeat with the prawns, if using. 3. Spray the air fryer basket with oil, and preheat the air fryer to 204ºC. Working in 2 or 3 batches, arrange the fish and prawns in a single layer in the basket, taking care not to crowd the basket. Spray with oil. Air fry for 5 minutes, then flip and air fry for another 4 to 5 minutes until the outside is brown and crisp and the inside of the fish is opaque and flakes easily with a fork. Repeat with the remaining seafood. 4. Place the fried seafood on a platter. Use a slotted spoon to remove the salsa criolla from the bowl, leaving behind any liquid that has accumulated. Place the salsa criolla on top of the fried seafood. Serve immediately with the remaining lime, cut into wedges, and mayonnaise or tartar sauce as desired.

Pesto Prawns with Wild Rice Pilaf

Prep time: 5 minutes | Cook time: 5 minutes | Serves 4

455 g medium prawns, peeled and deveined	1 lemon, sliced
	390 g cooked wild rice pilaf
60 g pesto sauce	

1. Preheat the air fryer to 182ºC. 2. In a medium bowl, toss the prawns with the pesto sauce until well coated. 3. Place the prawns in a single layer in the air fryer basket. Put the lemon slices over the prawns and roast for 5 minutes. 4. Remove the lemons and discard. Serve a quarter of the prawns over 100 g wild rice with some favorite steamed vegetables.

Herbed Prawns Pita

Prep time: 5 minutes | Cook time: 8 minutes | Serves 4

455 g medium prawns, peeled and deveined	¼ teaspoon black pepper
	4 whole wheat pitas
2 tablespoons olive oil	110 g feta cheese, crumbled
1 teaspoon dried oregano	75 g shredded lettuce
½ teaspoon dried thyme	1 tomato, diced
½ teaspoon garlic powder	45 g black olives, sliced
¼ teaspoon onion powder	1 lemon
½ teaspoon salt	

1. Preheat the oven to 192ºC. 2. In a medium bowl, combine the prawns with the olive oil, oregano, thyme, garlic powder, onion powder, salt, and black pepper. 3. Pour prawns in a single layer in the air fryer basket and roast for 6 to 8 minutes, or until cooked through. 4. Remove from the air fryer and divide into warmed pitas with feta, lettuce, tomato, olives, and a squeeze of lemon.

Popcorn Prawns

Prep time: 15 minutes | Cook time: 18 to 20 minutes | Serves 4

70 g plain flour, plus 2 tablespoons	deveined
½ teaspoon garlic powder	Olive oil for misting or cooking spray
1½ teaspoons Old Bay Seasoning	Coating:
½ teaspoon onion powder	180 g panko crumbs
120 ml beer, plus 2 tablespoons	1 teaspoon Old Bay Seasoning
340 g prawns, peeled and	½ teaspoon ground black pepper

1. In a large bowl, mix together the flour, garlic powder, Old Bay Seasoning, and onion powder. Stir in beer to blend. 2. Add prawns to batter and stir to coat. 3. Combine the coating ingredients in food processor and pulse to finely crush the crumbs. Transfer crumbs to shallow dish. 4. Preheat the air fryer to 200ºC. 5. Pour the prawns and batter into a colander to drain. Stir with a spoon to drain excess batter. 6. Working with a handful of prawns at a time, roll in crumbs and place on a cookie sheet. 7. Spray breaded prawns with oil or cooking spray and place all at once into air fryer basket. 8. Air fry for 5 minutes. Shake basket or stir and mist again with olive oil or spray. Cook 5 more minutes, shake basket again, and mist lightly again. Continue cooking 3 to 5 more minutes, until browned and crispy.

Lemon-Tarragon Fish en Papillote

Prep time: 10 minutes | Cook time: 15 minutes | Serves 2

2 tablespoons salted butter, melted	435 g julienned fennel, or 1 stalk julienned celery
1 tablespoon fresh lemon juice	75 g thinly sliced red bell pepper
½ teaspoon dried tarragon, crushed, or 2 sprigs fresh tarragon	2 cod fillets, 170 g each, thawed if frozen
1 teaspoon kosher or coarse sea salt	Vegetable oil spray
85 g julienned carrots	½ teaspoon black pepper

1. In a medium bowl, combine the butter, lemon juice, tarragon, and ½ teaspoon of the salt. Whisk well until you get a creamy sauce. Add the carrots, fennel, and bell pepper and toss to combine; set aside. 2. Cut two squares of baking paper each large enough to hold one fillet and half the vegetables. Spray the fillets with vegetable oil spray. Season both sides with the remaining ½ teaspoon salt and the black pepper. 3. Lay one fillet down on each baking paper square. Top each with half the vegetables. Pour any remaining sauce over the vegetables. 4. Fold over the baking paper and crimp the sides in small, tight folds to hold the fish, vegetables, and sauce securely inside the packet. Place the packets in the air fryer basket. Set the air fryer to 176ºC for 15 minutes. 5. Transfer each packet to a plate. Cut open with scissors just before serving (be careful, as the steam inside will be hot).

Firecracker Prawns

Prep time: 10 minutes | Cook time: 7 minutes | Serves 4

455 g medium prawns, peeled and deveined	2 tablespoons Sriracha
2 tablespoons salted butter, melted	¼ teaspoon powdered sweetener
½ teaspoon Old Bay seasoning	60 ml full-fat mayonnaise
¼ teaspoon garlic powder	⅛ teaspoon ground black pepper

1. In a large bowl, toss prawns in butter, Old Bay seasoning, and garlic powder. Place prawns into the air fryer basket. 2. Adjust the temperature to 204ºC and set the timer for 7 minutes. 3. Flip the prawns halfway through the cooking time. Prawns will be bright pink when fully cooked. 4. In another large bowl, mix Sriracha, sweetener, mayonnaise, and pepper. Toss prawns in the spicy mixture and serve immediately.

Sweet Tilapia Fillets

Prep time: 5 minutes | Cook time: 14 minutes | Serves 4

2 tablespoons granulated sweetener	vinegar
1 tablespoon apple cider	4 tilapia fillets, boneless
	1 teaspoon olive oil

1. Mix apple cider vinegar with olive oil and sweetener. 2. Then rub the tilapia fillets with the sweet mixture and put in the air fryer basket in one layer. Cook the fish at 182ºC for 7 minutes per side.

Honey-Balsamic Salmon

Prep time: 5 minutes | Cook time: 8 minutes | Serves 2

Olive or vegetable oil, for spraying	2 teaspoons red pepper flakes
2 (170 g) salmon fillets	2 teaspoons olive oil
60 ml balsamic vinegar	½ teaspoon salt
2 tablespoons honey	¼ teaspoon freshly ground black pepper

1. Line the air fryer basket with baking paper and spray lightly with oil. 2. Place the salmon in the prepared basket. 3. In a small bowl, whisk together the balsamic vinegar, honey, red pepper flakes, olive oil, salt, and black pepper. Brush the mixture over the salmon. 4. Roast at 200ºC for 7 to 8 minutes, or until the internal temperature reaches 64ºC. Serve immediately.

Sea Bass with Roasted Root Vegetables

Prep time: 10 minutes | Cook time: 15 minutes | Serves 4

1 carrot, diced small	4 sea bass fillets
1 parsnip, diced small	½ teaspoon onion powder
1 swede, diced small	2 garlic cloves, minced
60 ml olive oil	1 lemon, sliced, plus additional
1 teaspoon salt, divided	wedges for serving

1. Preheat the air fryer to 192°C. 2. In a small bowl, toss the carrot, parsnip, and swede with olive oil and 1 teaspoon salt. 3. Lightly season the sea bass with the remaining 1 teaspoon of salt and the onion powder, then place it into the air fryer basket in a single layer. 4. Spread the garlic over the top of each fillet, then cover with lemon slices. 5. Pour the prepared vegetables into the basket around and on top of the fish. Roast for 15 minutes. 6. Serve with additional lemon wedges if desired.

Apple Cider Mussels

Prep time: 10 minutes | Cook time: 2 minutes | Serves 5

900 g mussels, cleaned and de-bearded	1 teaspoon ground cumin
1 teaspoon onion powder	1 tablespoon avocado oil
	60 ml apple cider vinegar

1. Mix mussels with onion powder, ground cumin, avocado oil, and apple cider vinegar. 2. Put the mussels in the air fryer and cook at 202°C for 2 minutes.

Crunchy Fish Sticks

Prep time: 30 minutes | Cook time: 9 minutes | Serves 4

455 g cod fillets	black pepper, to taste
170 g finely ground blanched almond flour	60 ml mayonnaise
2 teaspoons Old Bay seasoning	1 large egg, beaten
½ teaspoon paprika	Avocado oil spray
Sea salt and freshly ground	Tartar sauce, for serving

1. Cut the fish into ¾-inch-wide strips. 2. In a shallow bowl, stir together the almond flour, Old Bay seasoning, paprika, and salt and pepper to taste. In another shallow bowl, whisk together the mayonnaise and egg. 3. Dip the cod strips in the egg mixture, then the almond flour, gently pressing with your fingers to help adhere to the coating. 4. Place the coated fish on a baking paper -lined baking sheet and freeze for 30 minutes. 5. Spray the air fryer basket with oil. Set the air fryer to 204°C. Place the fish in the basket in a single layer, and spray each piece with oil. 6. Cook for 5 minutes. Flip and spray with more oil. Cook for 4 minutes more, until the internal temperature reaches 60°C. Serve with the tartar sauce.

Crispy Prawns with Coriander

Prep time: 40 minutes | Cook time: 10 minutes | Serves 4

455 g raw large prawns, peeled and deveined with tails on or off	1 egg
	75 g bread crumbs
30 g chopped fresh coriander	Salt and freshly ground black pepper, to taste
Juice of 1 lime	Cooking oil spray
70 g plain flour	240 ml seafood sauce

1. Place the prawns in a resealable plastic bag and add the cilantro and lime juice. Seal the bag. Shake it to combine. Marinate the prawns in the refrigerator for 30 minutes. 2. Place the flour in a small bowl. 3. In another small bowl, beat the egg. 4. Place the bread crumbs in a third small bowl, season with salt and pepper, and stir to combine. 5. Insert the crisper plate into the basket and the basket into the unit. Preheat the unit to 204°C.6. Remove the prawns from the plastic bag. Dip each in the flour, the egg, and the bread crumbs to coat. Gently press the crumbs onto the prawns. 7. Once the unit is preheated, spray the crisper plate and the basket with cooking oil. Place the prawns in the basket. It is okay to stack them. Spray the prawns with the cooking oil. 8. Cook for 4 minutes, remove the basket and flip the prawns one at a time. Reinsert the basket to resume cooking. 10. When the cooking is complete, the prawns should be crisp. Let cool for 5 minutes. Serve with cocktail sauce.

Cod with Creamy Mustard Sauce

Prep time: 10 minutes | Cook time: 10 minutes | Serves 4

Fish:	½ teaspoon freshly ground
Olive or vegetable oil, for spraying	black pepper
	Mustard Sauce:
455 g cod fillets	120 ml heavy cream
2 tablespoons olive oil	3 tablespoons Dijon mustard
1 tablespoon lemon juice	1 tablespoon unsalted butter
1 teaspoon salt	1 teaspoon salt

Make the Fish: 1. Line the air fryer basket with baking paper and spray lightly with oil. 2. Rub the cod with the olive oil and lemon juice. Season with the salt and black pepper. 3. Place the cod in the prepared basket. You may need to work in batches, depending on the size of your air fryer. 4. Roast at 176°C for 5 minutes. Increase the temperature to 204°C and cook for another 5 minutes, until flaky and the internal temperature reaches 64°C. Make the Mustard Sauce: 5. In a small saucepan, mix together the heavy cream, mustard, butter, and salt and bring to a simmer over low heat. Cook for 3 to 4 minutes, or until the sauce starts to thicken. 6. Transfer the cod to a serving plate and drizzle with the mustard sauce. Serve immediately.

Panko Catfish Nuggets

Prep time: 10 minutes | Cook time: 7 to 8 minutes | Serves 4

2 medium catfish fillets, cut into chunks (approximately 1 × 2 inch)	2 tablespoons skimmed milk
	60 g cornflour
Salt and pepper, to taste	150 g panko bread crumbs
2 eggs	Cooking spray

1. Preheat the air fryer to 200°C. 2. In a medium bowl, season the fish chunks with salt and pepper to taste. 3. In a small bowl, beat together the eggs with milk until well combined. 4. Place the cornflour and bread crumbs into separate shallow dishes. 5. Dredge the fish chunks one at a time in the cornflour, coating well on both sides, then dip in the egg mixture, shaking off any excess, finally press well into the bread crumbs. Spritz the fish chunks with cooking spray. 6. Arrange the fish chunks in the air fryer basket in a single layer. You may need to cook in batches depending on the size of your air fryer basket. 7. Fry the fish chunks for 7 to 8 minutes until they are no longer translucent in the center and golden brown. Shake the basket once during cooking. 8. Remove the fish chunks from the basket to a plate. Repeat with the remaining fish chunks. 9. Serve warm.

Cheesy Tuna Patties

Prep time: 5 minutes | Cook time: 17 to 18 minutes | Serves 4

Tuna Patties:	pepper, to taste
455 g canned tuna, drained	1 tablespoon sesame oil
1 egg, whisked	Cheese Sauce:
2 tablespoons shallots, minced	1 tablespoon butter
1 garlic clove, minced	240 ml beer
1 cup grated Romano cheese	2 tablespoons grated Cheddar cheese
Sea salt and ground black	

1. Mix together the canned tuna, whisked egg, shallots, garlic, cheese, salt, and pepper in a large bowl and stir to incorporate. 2. Divide the tuna mixture into four equal portions and form each portion into a patty with your hands. Refrigerate the patties for 2 hours. 3. When ready, brush both sides of each patty with sesame oil. 4. Preheat the air fryer to 182°C. 5. Place the patties in the air fryer basket and bake for 14 minutes, flipping the patties halfway through, or until lightly browned and cooked through. 6. Meanwhile, melt the butter in a pan over medium heat. 7. Pour in the beer and whisk constantly, or until it begins to bubble. 8. Add the grated Colby cheese and mix well. Continue cooking for 3 to 4 minutes, or until the cheese melts. Remove the patties from the basket to a plate. Drizzle them with the cheese sauce and serve immediately.

Steamed Cod with Garlic and Swiss Chard

Prep time: 5 minutes | Cook time: 12 minutes | Serves 4

1 teaspoon salt	½ white onion, thinly sliced
½ teaspoon dried oregano	135 g Swiss chard, washed, stemmed, and torn into pieces
½ teaspoon dried thyme	
½ teaspoon garlic powder	60 ml olive oil
4 cod fillets	1 lemon, quartered

1. Preheat the air fryer to 192°C. 2. In a small bowl, whisk together the salt, oregano, thyme, and garlic powder. 3. Tear off four pieces of aluminum foil, with each sheet being large enough to envelop one cod fillet and a quarter of the vegetables. 4. Place a cod fillet in the middle of each sheet of foil, then sprinkle on all sides with the spice mixture. 5. In each foil packet, place a quarter of the onion slices and 30 g Swiss chard, then drizzle 1 tablespoon olive oil and squeeze ¼ lemon over the contents of each foil packet. 6. Fold and seal the sides of the foil packets and then place them into the air fryer basket. Steam for 12 minutes. 7. Remove from the basket, and carefully open each packet to avoid a steam burn.

Miso Salmon

Prep time: 10 minutes | Cook time: 12 minutes | Serves 2

2 tablespoons brown sugar	black pepper
2 tablespoons soy sauce	2 salmon fillets, 140 g each
2 tablespoons white miso paste	Vegetable oil spray
1 teaspoon minced garlic	1 teaspoon sesame seeds
1 teaspoon minced fresh ginger	2 spring onions, thinly sliced,
½ teaspoon freshly cracked	for garnish

1. In a small bowl, whisk together the brown sugar, soy sauce, miso, garlic, ginger, and pepper to combine. 2. Place the salmon fillets on a plate. Pour half the sauce over the fillets; turn the fillets to coat the other sides with sauce. 3. Spray the air fryer basket with vegetable oil spray. Place the sauce-covered salmon in the basket. Set the air fryer to 204°C for 12 minutes. Halfway through the cooking time, brush additional miso sauce on the salmon. 4. Sprinkle the salmon with the sesame seeds and spring onions and serve.

Tuna Steak

Prep time: 10 minutes | Cook time: 12 minutes | Serves 4

455 g tuna steaks, boneless and cubed	1 tablespoon avocado oil
	1 tablespoon apple cider vinegar
1 tablespoon mustard	

1. Mix avocado oil with mustard and apple cider vinegar. 2. Then brush tuna steaks with mustard mixture and put in the air fryer basket. 3. Cook the fish at 182°C for 6 minutes per side.

Crispy Fish Sticks

Prep time: 15 minutes | Cook time: 10 minutes | Serves 4

30 g crushed panko breadcrumbs
25 g blanched finely ground almond flour
½ teaspoon Old Bay seasoning

1 tablespoon coconut oil
1 large egg
455 g cod fillet, cut into ¾-inch strips

1. Place panko, almond flour, Old Bay seasoning, and coconut oil into a large bowl and mix together. In a medium bowl, whisk egg. 2. Dip each fish stick into the egg and then gently press into the flour mixture, coating as fully and evenly as possible. Place fish sticks into the air fryer basket. 3. Adjust the temperature to 204°C and air fry for 10 minutes or until golden. 4. Serve immediately.

Blackened Fish

Prep time: 15 minutes | Cook time: 8 minutes | Serves 4

1 large egg, beaten
Blackened seasoning, as needed
2 tablespoons light brown sugar

4 tilapia fillets, 110g each
Cooking spray

1. In a shallow bowl, place the beaten egg. In a second shallow bowl, stir together the Blackened seasoning and the brown sugar. 2. One at a time, dip the fish fillets in the egg, then the brown sugar mixture, coating thoroughly. 3. Preheat the air fryer to 150°C. Line the air fryer basket with baking paper. 4. Place the coated fish on the baking paper and spritz with oil. 5. Bake for 4 minutes. Flip the fish, spritz it with oil, and bake for 4 to 6 minutes more until the fish is white inside and flakes easily with a fork. 6. Serve immediately.

Thai Prawn Skewers with Peanut Dipping Sauce

Prep time: 15 minutes | Cook time: 6 minutes | Serves 2

Salt and pepper, to taste
340 g extra-large prawns, peeled and deveined
1 tablespoon vegetable oil
1 teaspoon honey
½ teaspoon grated lime zest plus 1 tablespoon juice, plus lime wedges for serving

6 (6-inch) wooden skewers
3 tablespoons creamy peanut butter
3 tablespoons hot tap water
1 tablespoon chopped fresh coriander
1 teaspoon fish sauce

1. Preheat the air fryer to 204°C. 2. Dissolve 2 tablespoons salt in 1 litre cold water in a large container. Add prawns, cover, and refrigerate for 15 minutes. 3. Remove prawns from brine and pat dry with paper towels. Whisk oil, honey, lime zest, and ¼ teaspoon pepper together in a large bowl. Add prawns and toss to coat. Thread prawns onto skewers, leaving about ¼ inch between each prawns (3 or 4 prawns per skewer). 4. Arrange 3 skewers in air fryer basket, parallel to each other and spaced evenly apart. Arrange remaining 3 skewers on top, perpendicular to the bottom layer. Air fry until prawns are opaque throughout, 6 to 8 minutes, flipping and rotating skewers halfway through cooking. 5. Whisk peanut butter, hot tap water, lime juice, coriander, and fish sauce together in a bowl until smooth. Serve skewers with peanut dipping sauce and lime wedges.

Fish Taco Bowl

Prep time: 10 minutes | Cook time: 12 minutes | Serves 4

½ teaspoon salt
¼ teaspoon garlic powder
¼ teaspoon ground cumin
4 cod fillets, 110 g each
360 g finely shredded green

cabbage
735 g mayonnaise
¼ teaspoon ground black pepper
20 g chopped pickled jalapeños

1. Sprinkle salt, garlic powder, and cumin over cod and place into ungreased air fryer basket. Adjust the temperature to 176°C and air fry for 12 minutes, turning fillets halfway through cooking. Cod will flake easily and have an internal temperature of at least 64°C when done. 2. In a large bowl, toss cabbage with mayonnaise, pepper, and jalapeños until fully coated. Serve cod warm over cabbage slaw on four medium plates.

Easy Scallops

Prep time: 5 minutes | Cook time: 4 minutes | Serves 2

12 medium sea scallops, rinsed and patted dry
1 teaspoon fine sea salt
¾ teaspoon ground black

pepper, plus more for garnish
Fresh thyme leaves, for garnish (optional)
Avocado oil spray

1. Preheat the air fryer to 200°C. Coat the air fryer basket with avocado oil spray. 2. Place the scallops in a medium bowl and spritz with avocado oil spray. Sprinkle the salt and pepper to season. 3. Transfer the seasoned scallops to the air fryer basket, spacing them apart. You may need to work in batches to avoid overcrowding. 4. Air fry for 4 minutes, flipping the scallops halfway through, or until the scallops are firm and reach an internal temperature of just 64°C on a meat thermometer. 5. Remove from the basket and repeat with the remaining scallops. 6. Sprinkle the pepper and thyme leaves on top for garnish, if desired. Serve immediately.

Tilapia Almondine

Prep time: 10 minutes | Cook time: 10 minutes | Serves 2

50 g almond flour or fine dried bread crumbs	salt
2 tablespoons salted butter or ghee, melted	60 g mayonnaise
	2 tilapia fillets
1 teaspoon black pepper	435 g thinly sliced almonds
½ teaspoon kosher or coarse sea	Vegetable oil spray

1. In a small bowl, mix together the almond flour, butter, pepper and salt. 2. Spread the mayonnaise on both sides of each fish fillet. Dredge the fillets in the almond flour mixture. Spread the sliced almonds on one side of each fillet, pressing lightly to adhere. 3. Spray the air fryer basket with vegetable oil spray. Place the fish fillets in the basket. Set the air fryer to 164ºC for 10 minutes, or until the fish flakes easily with a fork.

Garlic Lemon Scallops

Prep time: 5 minutes | Cook time: 10 minutes | Serves 4

4 tablespoons salted butter, melted	8 sea scallops, 30 g each, cleaned and patted dry
4 teaspoons peeled and finely minced garlic	¼ teaspoon salt
½ small lemon, zested and juiced	¼ teaspoon ground black pepper

1. In a small bowl, mix butter, garlic, lemon zest, and lemon juice. Place scallops in an ungreased round nonstick baking dish. Pour butter mixture over scallops, then sprinkle with salt and pepper. 2. Place dish into air fryer basket. Adjust the temperature to 182ºC and bake for 10 minutes. Scallops will be opaque and firm, and have an internal temperature of 56ºC when done. Serve warm.

Lemon-Pepper Trout

Prep time: 5 minutes | Cook time: 15 minutes | Serves 4

4 trout fillets	2 garlic cloves, sliced
2 tablespoons olive oil	1 lemon, sliced, plus additional wedges for serving
½ teaspoon salt	
1 teaspoon black pepper	

1. Preheat the air fryer to 192ºC. 2. Brush each fillet with olive oil on both sides and season with salt and pepper. Place the fillets in an even layer in the air fryer basket. 3. Place the sliced garlic over the tops of the trout fillets, then top the garlic with lemon slices and roast for 12 to 15 minutes, or until it has reached an internal temperature of 64ºC. 4. Serve with fresh lemon wedges.

Salmon with Cauliflower

Prep time: 10 minutes | Cook time: 25 minutes | Serves 4

455 g salmon fillet, diced	melted
100 g cauliflower, shredded	1 teaspoon ground turmeric
1 tablespoon dried coriander	60 ml coconut cream
1 tablespoon coconut oil,	

1. Mix salmon with cauliflower, dried cilantro, ground turmeric, coconut cream, and coconut oil. 2. Transfer the salmon mixture into the air fryer and cook the meal at 176ºC for 25 minutes. Stir the meal every 5 minutes to avoid the burning.

Chapter 8 Vegetables and Sides

Parmesan Herb Focaccia Bread

Prep time: 10 minutes | Cook time: 10 minutes | Serves 6

225 g shredded Mozzarella cheese

30 g) full-fat cream cheese

95 g blanched finely ground almond flour

40 g ground golden flaxseed

20 g grated Parmesan cheese

½ teaspoon bicarbonate of soda

2 large eggs

½ teaspoon garlic powder

¼ teaspoon dried basil

¼ teaspoon dried rosemary

2 tablespoons salted butter, melted and divided

1. Place Mozzarella, cream cheese, and almond flour into a large microwave-safe bowl and microwave for 1 minute. Add the flaxseed, Parmesan, and bicarbonate of soda and stir until smooth ball forms. If the mixture cools too much, it will be hard to mix. Return to microwave for 10 to 15 seconds to rewarm if necessary. 2. Stir in eggs. You may need to use your hands to get them fully incorporated. Just keep stirring and they will absorb into the dough. 3. Sprinkle dough with garlic powder, basil, and rosemary and knead into dough. Grease a baking pan with 1 tablespoon melted butter. Press the dough evenly into the pan. Place pan into the air fryer basket. 4. Adjust the temperature to 200°C and bake for 10 minutes. 5. At 7 minutes, cover with foil if bread begins to get too dark. 6. Remove and let cool at least 30 minutes. Drizzle with remaining butter and serve.

Shishito Pepper Roast

Prep time: 4 minutes | Cook time: 9 minutes | Serves 4

Cooking oil spray (sunflower, safflower, or refined coconut)

450 g shishito, Anaheim, or bell peppers, rinsed

1 tablespoon soy sauce

2 teaspoons freshly squeezed lime juice

2 large garlic cloves, pressed

1. Insert the crisper plate into the basket and the basket into the unit. Preheat the unit by selecting AIR ROAST, setting the temperature to 200°C, and setting the time to 3 minutes. Select START/STOP to begin. 2. Once the unit is preheated, spray the crisper plate and the basket with cooking oil. Place the peppers into the basket and spray them with oil. 3. Select AIR ROAST, set the temperature to 200°C, and set the time to 9 minutes. Select START/STOP to begin. 4. After 3 minutes, remove the basket and shake the peppers. Spray the peppers with more oil. Reinsert the basket to resume cooking. Repeat this step again after 3 minutes. 5. While the peppers roast,

in a medium bowl, whisk the soy sauce, lime juice, and garlic until combined. Set aside. 6. When the cooking is complete, several of the peppers should have lots of nice browned spots on them. If using Anaheim or bell peppers, cut a slit in the side of each pepper and remove the seeds, which can be bitter. 7. Place the roasted peppers in the bowl with the sauce. Toss to coat the peppers evenly and serve.

Parmesan-Thyme Butternut Squash

Prep time: 15 minutes | Cook time: 20 minutes | Serves 4

350 g butternut squash, cubed into 1-inch pieces (approximately 1 medium)

2 tablespoons olive oil

¼ teaspoon salt

¼ teaspoon garlic powder

¼ teaspoon black pepper

1 tablespoon fresh thyme

20 g grated Parmesan

1. Preheat the air fryer to 180°C. 2. In a large bowl, combine the cubed squash with the olive oil, salt, garlic powder, pepper, and thyme until the squash is well coated. 3. Pour this mixture into the air fryer basket, and roast for 10 minutes. Stir and roast another 8 to 10 minutes more. 4. Remove the squash from the air fryer and toss with freshly grated Parmesan before serving.

Tofu Bites

Prep time: 15 minutes | Cook time: 30 minutes | Serves 4

1 packaged firm tofu, cubed and pressed to remove excess water

1 tablespoon soy sauce

1 tablespoon ketchup

1 tablespoon maple syrup

½ teaspoon vinegar

1 teaspoon liquid smoke

1 teaspoon hot sauce

2 tablespoons sesame seeds

1 teaspoon garlic powder

Salt and ground black pepper, to taste

Cooking spray

1. Preheat the air fryer to 192°C. 2. Spritz a baking dish with cooking spray. 3. Combine all the ingredients to coat the tofu completely and allow the marinade to absorb for half an hour. 4. Transfer the tofu to the baking dish, then air fry for 15 minutes. Flip the tofu over and air fry for another 15 minutes on the other side. 5. Serve immediately.

Garlic Courgette and Red Peppers

Prep time: 5 minutes | Cook time: 15 minutes | Serves 6

2 medium courgette, cubed
1 red pepper, diced
2 garlic cloves, sliced
2 tablespoons olive oil
½ teaspoon salt

1. Preheat the air fryer to 193°C. 2. In a large bowl, mix together the courgette, bell pepper, and garlic with the olive oil and salt. 3. Pour the mixture into the air fryer basket, and roast for 7 minutes. Shake or stir, then roast for 7 to 8 minutes more.

Saltine Wax Beans

Prep time: 10 minutes | Cook time: 7 minutes | Serves 4

60 g flour
1 teaspoon smoky chipotle powder
½ teaspoon ground black pepper
1 teaspoon sea salt flakes
2 eggs, beaten
55 g crushed cream crackers
285 g wax beans
Cooking spray

1. Preheat the air fryer to 180°C. 2. Combine the flour, chipotle powder, black pepper, and salt in a bowl. Put the eggs in a second bowl. Put the crushed cream crackers in a third bowl. 3. Wash the beans with cold water and discard any tough strings. 4. Coat the beans with the flour mixture, before dipping them into the beaten egg. Cover them with the crushed cream crackers. 5. Spritz the beans with cooking spray. 6. Air fry for 4 minutes. Give the air fryer basket a good shake and continue to air fry for 3 minutes. Serve hot.

Sausage-Stuffed Mushroom Caps

Prep time: 10 minutes | Cook time: 8 minutes | Serves 2

6 large portobello mushroom caps
230 g Italian sausage
15 g chopped onion
2 tablespoons blanched finely ground almond flour
20 g grated Parmesan cheese
1 teaspoon minced fresh garlic

1. Use a spoon to hollow out each mushroom cap, reserving scrapings. 2. In a medium skillet over medium heat, brown the sausage about 10 minutes or until fully cooked and no pink remains. Drain and then add reserved mushroom scrapings, onion, almond flour, Parmesan, and garlic. Gently fold ingredients together and continue cooking an additional minute, then remove from heat. 3. Evenly spoon the mixture into mushroom caps and place the caps into a 6-inch round pan. Place pan into the air fryer basket. 4. Adjust the temperature to 192°C and set the timer for 8 minutes. 5. When finished cooking, the tops will be browned and bubbling. Serve warm.

Green Peas with Mint

Prep time: 5 minutes | Cook time: 5 minutes | Serves 4

75 g shredded lettuce
1 (280 g) package frozen green peas, thawed
1 tablespoon fresh mint, shredded
1 teaspoon melted butter

1. Lay the shredded lettuce in the air fryer basket. 2. Toss together the peas, mint, and melted butter and spoon over the lettuce. 3. Air fry at 180°C for 5 minutes, until peas are warm and lettuce wilts.

Southwestern Roasted Corn

Prep time: 10 minutes | Cook time: 10 minutes | Serves 4

Corn:
240 g thawed frozen corn kernels
50 g diced yellow onion
150 g mixed diced bell peppers
1 jalapeño, diced
1 tablespoon fresh lemon juice
1 teaspoon ground cumin
½ teaspoon ancho chili powder
½ teaspoon coarse sea salt
For Serving:
150 g queso fresco or feta cheese
10 g chopped fresh coriander
1 tablespoon fresh lemon juice

1. For the corn: In a large bowl, stir together the corn, onion, bell peppers, jalapeño, lemon juice, cumin, chili powder, and salt until well incorporated. 2. Pour the spiced vegetables into the air fryer basket. Set the air fryer to 192°C for 10 minutes, stirring halfway through the cooking time. 3. Transfer the corn mixture to a serving bowl. Add the cheese, coriander, and lemon juice and stir well to combine. Serve immediately.

Indian Aubergine Bharta

Prep time: 15 minutes | Cook time: 20 minutes | Serves 4

1 medium aubergine
2 tablespoons vegetable oil
25 g finely minced onion
100 g finely chopped fresh tomato
2 tablespoons fresh lemon juice
2 tablespoons chopped fresh coriander
½ teaspoon coarse sea salt
⅛ teaspoon cayenne pepper

1. Rub the aubergine all over with the vegetable oil. Place the aubergine in the air fryer basket. Set the air fryer to 200°C for 20 minutes, or until the aubergine skin is blistered and charred. 2. Transfer the aubergine to a re-sealable plastic bag, seal, and set aside for 15 to 20 minutes (the aubergine will finish cooking in the residual heat trapped in the bag). 3. Transfer the aubergine to a large bowl. Peel off and discard the charred skin. Roughly mash the aubergine flesh. Add the onion, tomato, lemon juice, coriander, salt, and cayenne. Stir to combine.

Sesame Taj Tofu

Prep time: 5 minutes | Cook time: 25 minutes | Serves 4

1 block firm tofu, pressed and cut into 1-inch thick cubes
2 tablespoons soy sauce
2 teaspoons toasted sesame seeds
1 teaspoon rice vinegar
1 tablespoon cornflour

1. Preheat the air fryer to 200°C. 2. Add the tofu, soy sauce, sesame seeds, and rice vinegar in a bowl together and mix well to coat the tofu cubes. Then cover the tofu in cornflour and put it in the air fryer basket. 3. Air fry for 25 minutes, giving the basket a shake at five-minute intervals to ensure the tofu cooks evenly. 4. Serve immediately.

Air Fried Potatoes with Olives

Prep time: 15 minutes | Cook time: 40 minutes | Serves 1

1 medium Maris Piper potatoes, scrubbed and peeled
1 teaspoon olive oil
¼ teaspoon onion powder
⅛ teaspoon salt
Dollop of butter
Dollop of cream cheese
1 tablespoon Kalamata olives
1 tablespoon chopped chives

1. Preheat the air fryer to 200°C. 2. In a bowl, coat the potatoes with the onion powder, salt, olive oil, and butter. 3. Transfer to the air fryer and air fry for 40 minutes, turning the potatoes over at the halfway point. 4. Take care when removing the potatoes from the air fryer and serve with the cream cheese, Kalamata olives and chives on top.

Breaded Green Tomatoes

Prep time: 15 minutes | Cook time: 30 minutes | Serves 4

60 g plain flour
2 eggs
60 g semolina
60 g panko bread crumbs
1 teaspoon garlic powder
Salt and freshly ground black pepper, to taste
2 green tomatoes, cut into ½-inch-thick rounds
Cooking oil spray

1. Place the flour in a small bowl. 2. In another small bowl, beat the eggs. 3. In a third small bowl, stir together the semolina, panko, and garlic powder. Season with salt and pepper. 4. Dip each tomato slice into the flour, the egg, and finally the semolina mixture to coat. 5. Insert the crisper plate into the basket and the basket into the unit. Preheat the unit by selecting AIR FRY, setting the temperature to 200°C, and setting the time to 3 minutes. Select START/STOP to begin. 6. Once the unit is preheated, spray the crisper plate and the basket with cooking oil. Working in batches, place the tomato slices in the air fryer in a single layer. Do not stack them. Spray the tomato slices with the cooking oil. 7. Select AIR

FRY, set the temperature to 200°C, and set the time to 10 minutes. Select START/STOP to begin. 8. After 5 minutes, use tongs to flip the tomatoes. Resume cooking for 4 to 5 minutes, or until crisp. 9. When the cooking is complete, transfer the fried green tomatoes to a plate. Repeat steps 6, 7, and 8 for the remaining tomatoes.

Easy Potato Croquettes

Prep time: 15 minutes | Cook time: 15 minutes | Serves 10

55 g nutritional yeast
300 g boiled potatoes, mashed
1 flax egg
1 tablespoon flour
2 tablespoons chopped chives
Salt and ground black pepper, to taste
2 tablespoons vegetable oil
30 g bread crumbs

1. Preheat the air fryer to 200°C. 2. In a bowl, combine the nutritional yeast, potatoes, flax egg, flour, and chives. Sprinkle with salt and pepper as desired. 3. In a separate bowl, mix the vegetable oil and bread crumbs to achieve a crumbly consistency. 4. Shape the potato mixture into small balls and dip each one into the bread crumb mixture. 5. Put the croquettes inside the air fryer and air fry for 15 minutes, ensuring the croquettes turn golden brown. 6. Serve immediately.

Asian Tofu Salad

Prep time: 25 minutes | Cook time: 15 minutes | Serves 2

Tofu:
1 tablespoon soy sauce
1 tablespoon vegetable oil
1 teaspoon minced fresh ginger
1 teaspoon minced garlic
230 g extra-firm tofu, drained and cubed
Salad:
60 ml rice vinegar
1 tablespoon sugar
1 teaspoon salt
1 teaspoon black pepper
25 g sliced spring onions
120 g julienned cucumber
50 g julienned red onion
130 g julienned carrots
6 butter lettuce leaves

1. For the tofu: In a small bowl, whisk together the soy sauce, vegetable oil, ginger, and garlic. Add the tofu and mix gently. Let stand at room temperature for 10 minutes. 2. Arrange the tofu in a single layer in the air fryer basket. Set the air fryer to 200°C for 15 minutes, shaking halfway through the cooking time. 3. Meanwhile, for the salad: In a large bowl, whisk together the vinegar, sugar, salt, pepper, and spring onions. Add the cucumber, onion, and carrots and toss to combine. Set aside to marinate while the tofu cooks. 4. To serve, arrange three lettuce leaves on each of two plates. Pile the marinated vegetables (and marinade) on the lettuce. Divide the tofu between the plates and serve.

Caramelized Aubergine with Harissa Yogurt

Prep time: 10 minutes | Cook time: 15 minutes | Serves 2

1 medium aubergine (about 340 g), cut crosswise into ½-inch-thick slices and quartered	ground black pepper, to taste
	120 g plain yogurt (not Greek)
2 tablespoons vegetable oil	2 tablespoons harissa paste
coarse sea salt and freshly	1 garlic clove, grated
	2 teaspoons honey

1. In a bowl, toss together the aubergine and oil, season with salt and pepper, and toss to coat evenly. Transfer to the air fryer and air fry at 200ºC, shaking the basket every 5 minutes, until the aubergine is caramelized and tender, about 15 minutes. 2. Meanwhile, in a small bowl, whisk together the yogurt, harissa, and garlic, then spread onto a serving plate. 3. Pile the warm aubergine over the yogurt and drizzle with the honey just before serving.

Buttery Mushrooms

Prep time: 10 minutes | Cook time: 10 minutes | Serves 4

230 g shitake mushrooms, halved	¼ teaspoon salt
	¼ teaspoon ground black pepper
2 tablespoons salted butter, melted	

1. In a medium bowl, toss mushrooms with butter, then sprinkle with salt and pepper. Place into ungreased air fryer basket. Adjust the temperature to 200ºCand air fry for 10 minutes, shaking the basket halfway through cooking. Mushrooms will be tender when done. Serve warm.

Lemony Broccoli

Prep time: 10 minutes | Cook time: 9 to 14 minutes per batch | Serves 4

1 large head broccoli, rinsed and patted dry	1 tablespoon freshly squeezed lemon juice
2 teaspoons extra-virgin olive oil	Olive oil spray

1. Cut off the broccoli florets and separate them. You can use the stems, too; peel the stems and cut them into 1-inch chunks. 2. Insert the crisper plate into the basket and the basket into the unit. Preheat the unit by selecting AIR ROAST, setting the temperature to 200ºC, and setting the time to 3 minutes. Select START/STOP to begin. 3. In a large bowl, toss together the broccoli, olive oil, and lemon juice until coated. 4. Once the unit is preheated, spray the crisper plate with olive oil. Working in batches, place half the broccoli into the basket. 5. Select AIR ROAST, set the temperature to 200ºC, and set the time to 14 minutes. Select START/STOP to begin. 6. After 5 minutes, remove the basket and shake the broccoli. Reinsert the basket to resume cooking. Check the broccoli after 5 minutes. If it is crisp-tender and slightly brown around the edges, it is done. If not, resume cooking. 7. When the cooking is complete, transfer the broccoli to a serving bowl. Repeat steps 5 and 6 with the remaining broccoli. Serve immediately.

Garlic Herb Radishes

Prep time: 10 minutes | Cook time: 10 minutes | Serves 4

450 g radishes	½ teaspoon dried parsley
2 tablespoons unsalted butter, melted	¼ teaspoon dried oregano
	¼ teaspoon ground black pepper
½ teaspoon garlic powder	

1. Remove roots from radishes and cut into quarters. 2. In a small bowl, add butter and seasonings. Toss the radishes in the herb butter and place into the air fryer basket. 3. Adjust the temperature to 180ºC and set the timer for 10 minutes. 4. Halfway through the cooking time, toss the radishes in the air fryer basket. Continue cooking until edges begin to turn brown. 5. Serve warm.

Parmesan and Herb Sweet Potatoes

Prep time: 10 minutes | Cook time: 18 minutes | Serves 4

2 large sweet potatoes, peeled and cubed	½ teaspoon salt
	2 tablespoons shredded Parmesan
65 ml olive oil	
1 teaspoon dried rosemary	

1. Preheat the air fryer to 180ºC. 2. In a large bowl, toss the sweet potatoes with the olive oil, rosemary, and salt. 3. Pour the potatoes into the air fryer basket and roast for 10 minutes, then stir the potatoes and sprinkle the Parmesan over the top. Continue roasting for 8 minutes more. 4. Serve hot and enjoy.

Roasted Aubergine

Prep time: 15 minutes | Cook time: 15 minutes | Serves 4

1 large aubergine	¼ teaspoon salt
2 tablespoons olive oil	½ teaspoon garlic powder

1. Remove top and bottom from aubergine. Slice aubergine into ¼-inch-thick round slices. 2. Brush slices with olive oil. Sprinkle with salt and garlic powder. Place aubergine slices into the air fryer basket. 3. Adjust the temperature to 200ºCand set the timer for 15 minutes. 4. Serve immediately.

Mediterranean Courgette Boats

Prep time: 5 minutes | Cook time: 10 minutes | Serves 4

1 large courgette, ends removed, halved lengthwise
6 grape tomatoes, quartered
¼ teaspoon salt
65 g feta cheese
1 tablespoon balsamic vinegar
1 tablespoon olive oil

1. Use a spoon to scoop out 2 tablespoons from centre of each courgette half, making just enough space to fill with tomatoes and feta. 2. Place tomatoes evenly in centres of courgette halves and sprinkle with salt. Place into ungreased air fryer basket. Adjust the temperature to 180ºC and roast for 10 minutes. When done, courgette will be tender. 3. Transfer boats to a serving tray and sprinkle with feta, then drizzle with vinegar and olive oil. Serve warm.

Five-Spice Roasted Sweet Potatoes

Prep time: 10 minutes | Cook time: 12 minutes | Serves 4

½ teaspoon ground cinnamon
¼ teaspoon ground cumin
¼ teaspoon paprika
1 teaspoon chili powder
⅛ teaspoon turmeric
½ teaspoon salt (optional)
Freshly ground black pepper, to taste
2 large sweet potatoes, peeled and cut into ¾-inch cubes
1 tablespoon olive oil

1. In a large bowl, mix together cinnamon, cumin, paprika, chili powder, turmeric, salt, and pepper to taste. 2. Add potatoes and stir well. 3. Drizzle the seasoned potatoes with the olive oil and stir until evenly coated. 4. Place seasoned potatoes in a baking pan or an ovenproof dish that fits inside your air fryer basket. 5. Cook for 6 minutes at 200ºC, stop, and stir well. 6. Cook for an additional 6 minutes.

Rosemary-Roasted Red Potatoes

Prep time: 5 minutes | Cook time: 20 minutes | Serves 6

450 g red potatoes, quartered
65 ml olive oil
½ teaspoon coarse sea salt
¼ teaspoon black pepper
1 garlic clove, minced
4 rosemary sprigs

1. Preheat the air fryer to 180ºC. 2. In a large bowl, toss the potatoes with the olive oil, salt, pepper, and garlic until well coated. 3. Pour the potatoes into the air fryer basket and top with the sprigs of rosemary. 4. Roast for 10 minutes, then stir or toss the potatoes and roast for 10 minutes more. 5. Remove the rosemary sprigs and serve the potatoes. Season with additional salt and pepper, if needed.

Lush Vegetable Salad

Prep time: 15 minutes | Cook time: 10 minutes | Serves 4

6 plum tomatoes, halved
2 large red onions, sliced
4 long red pepper, sliced
2 yellow pepper, sliced
6 cloves garlic, crushed
1 tablespoon extra-virgin olive
oil
1 teaspoon paprika
½ lemon, juiced
Salt and ground black pepper, to taste
1 tablespoon baby capers

1. Preheat the air fryer to 220ºC. 2. Put the tomatoes, onions, peppers, and garlic in a large bowl and cover with the extra-virgin olive oil, paprika, and lemon juice. Sprinkle with salt and pepper as desired. 3. Line the inside of the air fryer basket with aluminum foil. Put the vegetables inside and air fry for 10 minutes, ensuring the edges turn brown. 4. Serve in a salad bowl with the baby capers.

Rosemary New Potatoes

Prep time: 10 minutes | Cook time: 5 to 6 minutes | Serves 4

3 large red potatoes
¼ teaspoon ground rosemary
¼ teaspoon ground thyme
⅛ teaspoon salt
⅛ teaspoon ground black pepper
2 teaspoons extra-light olive oil

1. Preheat the air fryer to 170ºC. 2. Place potatoes in large bowl and sprinkle with rosemary, thyme, salt, and pepper. 3. Stir with a spoon to distribute seasonings evenly. 4. Add oil to potatoes and stir again to coat well. 5. Air fry at 170ºC for 4 minutes. Stir and break apart any that have stuck together. 6. Cook an additional 1 to 2 minutes or until fork-tender.

Corn Croquettes

Prep time: 10 minutes | Cook time: 12 to 14 minutes | Serves 4

105 g leftover mashed potatoes
340 g corn kernels (if frozen, thawed, and well drained)
¼ teaspoon onion powder
⅛ teaspoon ground black
pepper
¼ teaspoon salt
50 g panko bread crumbs
Oil for misting or cooking spray

1. Place the potatoes and half the corn in food processor and pulse until corn is well chopped. 2. Transfer mixture to large bowl and stir in remaining corn, onion powder, pepper and salt. 3. Shape mixture into 16 balls. 4. Roll balls in panko crumbs, mist with oil or cooking spray, and place in air fryer basket. 5. Air fry at 180ºC for 12 to 14 minutes, until golden brown and crispy

Golden Garlicky Mushrooms

Prep time: 10 minutes | Cook time: 10 minutes | Serves 4

6 small mushrooms

1 tablespoon bread crumbs

1 tablespoon olive oil

30 g onion, peeled and diced

1 teaspoon parsley

1 teaspoon garlic purée

Salt and ground black pepper, to taste

1. Preheat the air fryer to 180ºC. 2. Combine the bread crumbs, oil, onion, parsley, salt, pepper and garlic in a bowl. Cut out the mushrooms' stalks and stuff each cap with the crumb mixture. 3. Air fry in the air fryer for 10 minutes. 4. Serve hot.

Turnip Fries

Prep time: 10 minutes | Cook time: 20 to 30 minutes | Serves 4

900 g turnip, peeled and cut into ¼ to ½-inch fries

2 tablespoons olive oil

Salt and freshly ground black pepper, to taste

1. Preheat the air fryer to 200ºC. 2. In a large bowl, combine the turnip and olive oil. Season to taste with salt and black pepper. Toss gently until thoroughly coated. 3. Working in batches if necessary, spread the turnip in a single layer in the air fryer basket. Pausing halfway through the cooking time to shake the basket, air fry for 20 to 30 minutes until the fries are lightly browned and crunchy.

Broccoli with Sesame Dressing

Prep time: 5 minutes | Cook time: 10 minutes | Serves 4

425 g broccoli florets, cut into bite-size pieces

1 tablespoon olive oil

¼ teaspoon salt

2 tablespoons sesame seeds

2 tablespoons rice vinegar

2 tablespoons coconut aminos

2 tablespoons sesame oil

½ teaspoon xylitol

¼ teaspoon red pepper flakes (optional)

1. Preheat the air fryer to 200ºC. 2. In a large bowl, toss the broccoli with the olive oil and salt until thoroughly coated. 3. Transfer the broccoli to the air fryer basket. Pausing halfway through the cooking time to shake the basket, air fry for 10 minutes until the stems are tender and the edges are beginning to crisp. 4. Meanwhile, in the same large bowl, whisk together the sesame seeds, vinegar, coconut aminos, sesame oil, xylitol, and red pepper flakes (if using). 5. Transfer the broccoli to the bowl and toss until thoroughly coated with the seasonings. Serve warm or at room temperature.

Chapter 9 Desserts

Chickpea Brownies

Prep time: 10 minutes | Cook time: 20 minutes | Serves 6

Vegetable oil

425 g can chickpeas, drained and rinsed

4 large eggs

80 ml coconut oil, melted

80 ml honey

3 tablespoons unsweetened

cocoa powder

1 tablespoon espresso powder (optional)

1 teaspoon baking powder

1 teaspoon baking soda

80 g chocolate chips

1. Preheat the air fryer to 164°C. 2. Generously grease a baking pan with vegetable oil. 3. In a blender or food processor, combine the chickpeas, eggs, coconut oil, honey, cocoa powder, espresso powder (if using), baking powder, and baking soda. Blend or process until smooth. Transfer to the prepared pan and stir in the chocolate chips by hand. 4. Set the pan in the air fryer basket and bake for 20 minutes, or until a toothpick inserted into the center comes out clean. 5. Let cool in the pan on a wire rack for 30 minutes before cutting into squares. 6. Serve immediately.

Boston Cream Donut Holes

Prep time: 30 minutes | Cook time: 4 minutes per batch | Makes 24 donut holes

200 g bread flour

1 teaspoon active dry yeast

1 tablespoon granulated sugar

¼ teaspoon salt

120 ml warm milk

½ teaspoon pure vanilla extract

2 egg yolks

2 tablespoons unsalted butter, melted

Vegetable oil

Custard Filling:

95 g box French vanilla instant pudding mix

175 ml whole milk

60 ml heavy cream

Chocolate Glaze:

170 g chocolate chips

80 ml heavy cream

1. Combine the flour, yeast, sugar, and salt in the bowl of a stand mixer. Add the milk, vanilla, egg yolks and butter. Mix until the dough starts to come together in a ball. Transfer the dough to a floured surface and knead the dough by hand for 2 minutes. Shape the dough into a ball, place it in a large, oiled bowl, cover the bowl with a clean kitchen towel and let the dough rise for 1 to 1½ hours or until the dough has doubled in size. 2. When the dough has risen, punch it down and roll it into a 24-inch log. Cut the dough into 24 pieces and roll each piece into a ball. Place the dough balls on a baking sheet and let them rise for another 30 minutes. 3. Preheat the air fryer to 204°C. 4. Spray or brush the dough balls lightly with vegetable oil and air fry eight at a time for 4 minutes, turning them over halfway through the cooking time. 5. While donut holes are cooking, make the filling and chocolate glaze. Make the filling: Use an electric hand mixer to beat the French vanilla pudding, milk and ¼ cup of heavy cream together for 2 minutes. 6. Make the chocolate glaze: Place the chocolate chips in a medium-sized bowl. Bring the heavy cream to a boil on the stovetop and pour it over the chocolate chips. Stir until the chips are melted and the glaze is smooth. 7. To fill the donut holes, place the custard filling in a pastry bag with a long tip. Poke a hole into the side of the donut hole with a small knife. Wiggle the knife around to make room for the filling. Place the pastry bag tip into the hole and slowly squeeze the custard into the center of the donut. Dip the top half of the donut into the chocolate glaze, letting any excess glaze drip back into the bowl. Let the glazed donut holes sit for a few minutes before serving

Crumbly Coconut-Pecan Cookies

Prep time: 10 minutes | Cook time: 25 minutes | Serves 10

170 g coconut flour

170 g extra-fine almond flour

½ teaspoon baking powder

⅓ teaspoon baking soda

3 eggs plus an egg yolk, beaten

175 ml coconut oil, at room temperature

125 g unsalted pecan nuts, roughly chopped

150 g monk fruit, or equivalent sweetener

¼ teaspoon freshly grated nutmeg

⅓ teaspoon ground cloves

½ teaspoon pure vanilla extract

½ teaspoon pure coconut extract

⅛ teaspoon fine sea salt

1. Preheat the air fryer to 188°C. Line the air fryer basket with baking paper. 2. Mix the coconut flour, almond flour, baking powder, and baking soda in a large mixing bowl. 3. In another mixing bowl, stir together the eggs and coconut oil. Add the wet mixture to the dry mixture. 4. Mix in the remaining ingredients and stir until a soft dough forms. 5. Drop about 2 tablespoons of dough on the baking paper for each cookie and flatten each biscuit until it's 1 inch thick. 6. Bake for about 25 minutes until the cookies are golden and firm to the touch. Remove from the basket to a plate. Let the cookies cool to room temperature and serve.

Spiced Apple Cake

Prep time: 15 minutes | Cook time: 30 minutes | Serves 6

Vegetable oil	1 tablespoon apple pie spice
2 diced & peeled Gala apples	½ teaspoon ground ginger
1 tablespoon fresh lemon juice	¼ teaspoon ground cardamom
55 g unsalted butter, softened	¼ teaspoon ground nutmeg
65 g granulated sugar	½ teaspoon kosher, or coarse
2 large eggs	sea salt
155 g plain flour	60 ml whole milk
1½ teaspoons baking powder	Icing sugar, for dusting

1. Grease a 0.7-liter Bundt, or tube pan with oil; set aside. 2. In a medium bowl, toss the apples with the lemon juice until well coated; set aside. 3. In a large bowl, combine the butter and sugar. Beat with an electric hand mixer on medium speed until the sugar has dissolved. Add the eggs and beat until fluffy. Add the flour, baking powder, apple pie spice, ginger, cardamom, nutmeg, salt, and milk. Mix until the batter is thick but pourable. 4. Pour the batter into the prepared pan. Top batter evenly with the apple mixture. Place the pan in the air fryer basket. Set the air fryer to 176°C and cook for 30 minutes, or until a toothpick inserted in the center of the cake comes out clean. Close the air fryer and let the cake rest for 10 minutes. Turn the cake out onto a wire rack and cool completely. 5. Right before serving, dust the cake with icing sugar.

Fried Cheesecake Bites

Prep time: 30 minutes | Cook time: 2 minutes | Makes 16 bites

225 g cream cheese, softened	divided
50 g powdered sweetener, plus	½ teaspoon vanilla extract
2 tablespoons, divided	50 g almond flour
4 tablespoons heavy cream,	

1. In a stand mixer fitted with a paddle attachment, beat the cream cheese, 50 g of the sweetener, 2 tablespoons of the heavy cream, and the vanilla until smooth. Using a small ice-cream scoop, divide the mixture into 16 balls and arrange them on a rimmed baking sheet lined with baking paper. Freeze for 45 minutes until firm. 2. Line the air fryer basket with baking paper and preheat the air fryer to 176°C. 3. In a small shallow bowl, combine the almond flour with the remaining 2 tablespoons of sweetener. 4. In another small shallow bowl, place the remaining 2 tablespoons cream. 5. One at a time, dip the frozen cheesecake balls into the cream and then roll in the almond flour mixture, pressing lightly to form an even coating. Arrange the balls in a single layer in the air fryer basket, leaving room between them. Air fry for 2 minutes until the coating is lightly browned.

Cream Cheese Danish

Prep time: 20 minutes | Cook time: 15 minutes | Serves 6

70 g blanched finely ground almond flour	2 large egg yolks
225 g shredded Mozzarella cheese	75 g powdered sweetener, divided
140 g full-fat cream cheese, divided	2 teaspoons vanilla extract, divided

1. In a large microwave-safe bowl, add almond flour, Mozzarella, and 30 g cream cheese. Mix and then microwave for 1 minute. 2. Stir and add egg yolks to the bowl. Continue stirring until soft dough forms. Add 50 g sweetener to dough and 1 teaspoon vanilla. 3. Cut a piece of baking paper to fit your air fryer basket. Wet your hands with warm water and press out the dough into a ¼-inch-thick rectangle. 4. In a medium bowl, mix remaining cream cheese, remaining sweetener, and vanilla. Place this cream cheese mixture on the right half of the dough rectangle. Fold over the left side of the dough and press to seal. Place into the air fryer basket. 5. Adjust the temperature to 164°C and bake for 15 minutes. 6. After 7 minutes, flip over the Danish. 7. When done, remove the Danish from baking paper and allow to completely cool before cutting.

Pumpkin-Spice Bread Pudding

Prep time: 15 minutes | Cook time: 35 minutes | Serves 6

Bread Pudding:	1/3 loaf of day-old baguette or
175 ml heavy whipping cream	crusty country bread, cubed
120 g canned pumpkin	4 tablespoons unsalted butter,
80 ml whole milk	melted
65 g granulated sugar	Sauce:
1 large egg plus 1 yolk	80 ml pure maple syrup
½ teaspoon pumpkin pie spice	1 tablespoon unsalted butter
⅛ teaspoon kosher, or coarse	120 ml heavy whipping cream
sea salt	½ teaspoon pure vanilla extract

1. For the bread pudding: In a medium bowl, combine the cream, pumpkin, milk, sugar, egg and yolk, pumpkin pie spice, and salt. Whisk until well combined. 2. In a large bowl, toss the bread cubes with the melted butter. Add the pumpkin mixture and gently toss until the ingredients are well combined. 3. Transfer the mixture to a baking pan. Place the pan in the air fryer basket. Set the fryer to 176°C cooking for 35 minutes, or until custard is set in the middle. 4. Meanwhile, for the sauce: In a small saucepan, combine the syrup and butter. Heat over medium heat, stirring, until the butter melts. Stir in the cream and simmer, stirring often, until the sauce has thickened, about 15 minutes. Stir in the vanilla. Remove the pudding from the air fryer. 5. Let the pudding stand for 10 minutes before serving with the warm sauce.

Vanilla Pound Cake

Prep time: 10 minutes | Cook time: 25 minutes | Serves 6

110 g blanched finely ground almond flour	1 teaspoon baking powder
55 g salted butter, melted	120 ml full-fat sour cream
100 g granulated sweetener	30 g full-fat cream cheese, softened
1 teaspoon vanilla extract	2 large eggs

1. In a large bowl, mix almond flour, butter, and sweetener. 2. Add in vanilla, baking powder, sour cream, and cream cheese and mix until well combined. Add eggs and mix. 3. Pour batter into a round baking pan. Place pan into the air fryer basket. 4. Adjust the temperature to 148ºC and bake for 25 minutes. 5. When the cake is done, a toothpick inserted in center will come out clean. The center should not feel wet. Allow it to cool completely, or the cake will crumble when moved.

Apple Dutch Baby

Prep time: 30 minutes | Cook time: 16 minutes |
Serves 2 to 3

Batter:	Apples:
2 large eggs	2 tablespoon butter
30 g plain flour	4 tablespoons granulated sugar
¼ teaspoon baking powder	¼ teaspoon ground cinnamon
1½ teaspoons granulated sugar	¼ teaspoon ground nutmeg
Pinch kosher, or coarse sea salt	1 small tart apple (such as
120 ml whole milk	Granny Smith), peeled, cored,
1 tablespoon butter, melted	and sliced
½ teaspoon pure vanilla extract	Vanilla ice cream (optional), for
¼ teaspoon ground nutmeg	serving

1. For the batter: In a medium bowl, combine the eggs, flour, baking powder, sugar, and salt. Whisk lightly. While whisking continuously, slowly pour in the milk. Whisk in the melted butter, vanilla, and nutmeg. Let the batter stand for 30 minutes. (You can also cover and refrigerate overnight.) 2. For the apples: Place the butter in a baking pan. Place the pan in the air fryer basket. Set the air fryer to 204ºC and cook for 2 minutes. In a small bowl, combine 2 tablespoons of the sugar with the cinnamon and nutmeg and stir until well combined. 3. When the pan is hot and the butter is melted, brush some butter up the sides of the pan. Sprinkle the spiced sugar mixture over the butter. Arrange the apple slices in the pan in a single layer and sprinkle the remaining 2 tablespoons sugar over the apples. Keep the air fryer at 204ºC and cook for a further2 minutes, or until the mixture bubbles. 4. Gently pour the batter over the apples. Set the air fryer to 176ºC cooking for 12 minutes, or until the pancake is golden brown around the edges, the center is cooked through, and a toothpick emerges clean. 5. Serve immediately with ice cream, if desired.

Butter Flax Cookies

Prep time: 25 minutes | Cook time: 20 minutes | Serves 4

225 g almond meal	A pinch of coarse salt
2 tablespoons flaxseed meal	1 large egg, room temperature.
30 g monk fruit, or equivalent sweetener	110 g unsalted butter, room temperature
1 teaspoon baking powder	1 teaspoon vanilla extract
A pinch of grated nutmeg	

1. Mix the almond meal, flaxseed meal, monk fruit, baking powder, grated nutmeg, and salt in a bowl. 2. In a separate bowl, whisk the egg, butter, and vanilla extract. 3. Stir the egg mixture into dry mixture; mix to combine well or until it forms a nice, soft dough. 4. Roll your dough out and cut out with a cookie cutter of your choice. Bake in the preheated air fryer at 176ºC for 10 minutes. Decrease the temperature to 164ºC and cook for 10 minutes longer. Bon appétit!

Almond-Roasted Pears

Prep time: 10 minutes | Cook time: 15 to 20 minutes
| Serves 4

Yogurt Topping:	2 whole pears
140-170 g pot vanilla Greek yogurt	4 crushed Biscoff biscuits
¼ teaspoon almond flavoring	1 tablespoon flaked almonds
	1 tablespoon unsalted butter

1. Stir the almond flavoring into yogurt and set aside while preparing pears. 2. Halve each pear and spoon out the core. 3. Place pear halves in air fryer basket, skin side down. 4. Stir together the crushed biscuits and almonds. Place a quarter of this mixture into the hollow of each pear half. 5. Cut butter into 4 pieces and place one piece on top of biscuit mixture in each pear. 6. Roast at 184ºC for 15 to 20 minutes, or until pears have cooked through but are still slightly firm. 7. Serve pears warm with a dollop of yogurt topping.

Coconut Macaroons

Prep time: 5 minutes | Cook time: 8 to 10 minutes |
Makes 12 macaroons

120 g desiccated, sweetened coconut	2 tablespoons sugar
	1 egg white
4½ teaspoons plain flour	½ teaspoon almond extract

1. Preheat the air fryer to 164ºC. 2. In a medium bowl, mix all ingredients together. 3. Shape coconut mixture into 12 balls. 4. Place all 12 macaroons in air fryer basket. They won't expand, so you can place them close together, but they shouldn't touch. 5. Air fry for 8 to 10 minutes, until golden.

Kentucky Chocolate Nut Pie

Prep time: 20 minutes | Cook time: 25 minutes | Serves 8

2 large eggs, beaten
75 g unsalted butter, melted
200 g granulated sugar
60 g plain flour
190 g coarsely chopped pecans

170 g milk chocolate chips
2 tablespoons bourbon, or peach juice
1 (9-inch) unbaked piecrust

1. In a large bowl, stir together the eggs and melted butter. Add the sugar and flour and stir until combined. Stir in the pecans, chocolate chips, and bourbon until well mixed. 2. Using a fork, prick holes in the bottom and sides of the pie crust. Pour the pie filling into the crust. 3. Preheat the air fryer to 176ºC. 4. Cook for 25 minutes, or until a knife inserted into the middle of the pie comes out clean. Let set for 5 minutes before serving.

Lime Bars

Prep time: 10 minutes | Cook time: 33 minutes | Makes 12 bars

140 g blanched finely ground almond flour, divided
75 g powdered sweetener, divided

4 tablespoons salted butter, melted
120 ml fresh lime juice
2 large eggs, whisked

1. In a medium bowl, mix together 110 g flour, 25 g sweetener, and butter. Press mixture into bottom of an ungreased round nonstick cake pan. 2. Place pan into air fryer basket. Adjust the temperature to 148ºC and bake for 13 minutes. Crust will be brown and set in the middle when done. 3. Allow to cool in pan 10 minutes. 4. In a medium bowl, combine remaining flour, remaining sweetener, lime juice, and eggs. Pour mixture over cooled crust and return to air fryer for 20 minutes. Top will be browned and firm when done. 5. Let cool completely in pan, about 30 minutes, then chill covered in the refrigerator 1 hour. Serve chilled.

Caramelized Fruit Skewers

Prep time: 10 minutes | Cook time: 3 to 5 minutes | Serves 4

2 peaches, peeled, pitted, and thickly sliced
3 plums, halved and pitted
3 nectarines, halved and pitted
1 tablespoon honey

½ teaspoon ground cinnamon
¼ teaspoon ground allspice
Pinch cayenne pepper
Special Equipment:
8 metal skewers

1. Preheat the air fryer to 204ºC. 2. Thread, alternating peaches, plums, and nectarines, onto the metal skewers that fit into the air fryer. 3. Thoroughly combine the honey, cinnamon, allspice, and cayenne in a small bowl. Brush the glaze generously over the fruit skewers. 4. Transfer the fruit skewers to the air fryer basket. You may need to cook in batches to avoid overcrowding. 5. Air fry for 3 to 5 minutes, or until the fruit is caramelized. 6. Remove from the basket and repeat with the remaining fruit skewers. 7. Let the fruit skewers rest for 5 minutes before serving.

Baked Cheesecake

Prep time: 30 minutes | Cook time: 35 minutes | Serves 6

50 g almond flour
1½ tablespoons unsalted butter, melted
2 tablespoons granulated sweetener
225 g cream cheese, softened
25 g powdered sweetener

½ teaspoon vanilla paste
1 egg, at room temperature
Topping:
355 ml sour cream
3 tablespoons powdered sweetener
1 teaspoon vanilla extract

1. Thoroughly combine the almond flour, butter, and 2 tablespoons of granulated sweetener in a mixing bowl. Press the mixture into the bottom of lightly greased custard cups. 2. Then, mix the cream cheese, 25 g of powdered sweetener, vanilla, and egg using an electric mixer on low speed. Pour the batter into the pan, covering the crust. 3. Bake in the preheated air fryer at 164ºC for 35 minutes until edges are puffed and the surface is firm. 4. Mix the sour cream, 3 tablespoons of powdered sweetener, and vanilla for the topping; spread over the crust and allow it to cool to room temperature. 5. Transfer to your refrigerator for 6 to 8 hours. Serve well chilled.

Grilled Peaches

Prep time: 5 minutes | Cook time: 10 minutes | Serves 4

Coconut, or avocado oil, for spraying
25 g crushed digestive biscuits
50 g packed light brown sugar
8 tablespoons unsalted butter

¼ teaspoon cinnamon
2 peaches, pitted and cut into quarters
4 scoops vanilla ice cream

1. Line the air fryer basket with baking paper, and spray lightly with oil. 2. In a small bowl, mix together the crushed biscuits, brown sugar, butter, and cinnamon with a fork until crumbly. 3. Place the peach wedges in the prepared basket, skin-side up. You may need to work in batches, depending on the size of your air fryer. 4. Air fry at 176ºC for 5 minutes, flip, and sprinkle with a spoonful of the biscuit mixture. Cook for another 5 minutes, or until tender and caramelized. 5. Top with a scoop of vanilla ice cream and any remaining crumble mixture. Serve immediately.

Oatmeal Raisin Bars

Prep time: 15 minutes | Cook time: 15 minutes | Serves 8

40 g plain flour

¼ teaspoon kosher, or coarse sea salt

¼ teaspoon baking powder

¼ teaspoon ground cinnamon

50 g light brown sugar, lightly packed

50 g granulated sugar

120 ml canola, or rapeseed oil

1 large egg

1 teaspoon vanilla extract

110 g quick-cooking oats

60 g raisins

1. Preheat the air fryer to 184ºC. 2. In a large bowl, combine the plain flour, kosher salt, baking powder, ground cinnamon, light brown sugar, granulated sugar, canola oil, egg, vanilla extract, quick-cooking oats, and raisins. 3. Spray a baking pan with nonstick cooking spray, then pour the oat mixture into the pan and press down to evenly distribute. Place the pan in the air fryer and bake for 15 minutes or until golden brown. 4. Remove from the air fryer and allow to cool in the pan on a wire rack for 20 minutes before slicing and serving.

Halle Berries-and-Cream Cobbler

Prep time: 10 minutes | Cook time: 25 minutes | Serves 4

340 g cream cheese, softened

1 large egg

75 g powdered sweetener

½ teaspoon vanilla extract

¼ teaspoon fine sea salt

120 g sliced fresh raspberries or strawberries

Biscuits:

3 large egg whites

70 g blanched almond flour

1 teaspoon baking powder

2½ tablespoons very cold

unsalted butter, cut into pieces

¼ teaspoon fine sea salt

Frosting:

55 g cream cheese, softened

1 tablespoon powdered sweetener

1 tablespoon unsweetened, unflavored almond milk or heavy cream

Fresh raspberries or strawberries, for garnish

1. Preheat the air fryer to 204ºC. Grease a pie pan. 2. In a large mixing bowl, use a hand mixer to combine the cream cheese, egg, and sweetener until smooth. Stir in the vanilla and salt. Gently fold in the raspberries with a rubber spatula. Pour the mixture into the prepared pan and set aside. 3. Make the biscuits: Place the egg whites in a medium-sized mixing bowl or the bowl of a stand mixer. Using a hand mixer or stand mixer, whip the egg whites until very fluffy and stiff. 4. In a separate medium-sized bowl, combine the almond flour and baking powder. Cut in the butter and add the salt, stirring gently to keep the butter pieces intact. 5. Gently fold the almond flour mixture into the egg whites. Use a large spoon or ice cream scooper to scoop out the dough and form it into a 2-inch-wide biscuit, making sure the butter stays in separate clumps. Place the biscuit on top of the raspberry mixture in the pan. Repeat with remaining dough to make 4 biscuits. 6. Place the pan in the air fryer and bake for 5 minutes, then lower the temperature to 164ºC and bake for another 17 to 20 minutes, until the biscuits are golden brown. 7. While the cobbler cooks, make the frosting: Place the cream cheese in a small bowl and stir to break it up. Add the sweetener and stir. Add the almond milk and stir until well combined. If you prefer a thinner frosting, add more almond milk. 8. Remove the cobbler from the air fryer and allow to cool slightly, then drizzle with the frosting. Garnish with fresh raspberries. 9. Store leftovers in an airtight container in the refrigerator for up to 3 days. Reheat the cobbler in a preheated 176ºC air fryer for 3 minutes, or until warmed through.

Chocolate Bread Pudding

Prep time: 10 minutes | Cook time: 10 to 12 minutes | Serves 4

Nonstick, flour-infused baking spray

1 egg

1 egg yolk

175 ml chocolate milk

2 tablespoons cocoa powder

3 tablespoons light brown sugar

3 tablespoons peanut butter

1 teaspoon vanilla extract

5 slices firm white bread, cubed

1. Spray a 6-by-2-inch round baking pan with the baking spray. Set aside. 2. In a medium bowl, whisk the egg, egg yolk, chocolate milk, cocoa powder, brown sugar, peanut butter, and vanilla until thoroughly combined. Stir in the bread cubes and let soak for 10 minutes. Spoon this mixture into the prepared pan. 3. Insert the crisper plate into the basket and the basket into the unit. Preheat the unit to 164ºC. 4. cook the pudding for about 10 minutes and then check if done. It is done when it is firm to the touch. If not, resume cooking. 5. When the cooking is complete, let the pudding cool for 5 minutes. Serve warm.

Berry Crumble

Prep time: 10 minutes | Cook time: 15 minutes | Serves 4

For the Filling:

300 g mixed berries

2 tablespoons sugar

1 tablespoon cornflour

1 tablespoon fresh lemon juice

For the Topping:

30 g plain flour

20 g rolled oats

1 tablespoon granulated sugar

2 tablespoons cold unsalted butter, cut into small cubes

Whipped cream or ice cream (optional)

1. Preheat the air fryer to 204ºC. 2. For the filling: In a round baking pan, gently mix the berries, sugar, cornflour, and lemon juice until thoroughly combined. 3. For the topping: In a small bowl, combine the flour, oats, and sugar. Stir the butter into the flour mixture until the mixture has the consistency of breadcrumbs. 4. Sprinkle the topping over the berries. 5. Put the pan in the air fryer basket and air fry for 15 minutes. Let cool for 5 minutes on a wire rack. 6. Serve topped with whipped cream or ice cream, if desired.

Hazelnut Butter Cookies

Prep time: 30 minutes | Cook time: 20 minutes | Serves 10

4 tablespoons liquid monk fruit, or agave syrup	190 g almond flour
65 g hazelnuts, ground	110 g coconut flour
110 g unsalted butter, room temperature	55 g granulated sweetener
	2 teaspoons ground cinnamon

1. Firstly, cream liquid monk fruit with butter until the mixture becomes fluffy. Sift in both types of flour. 2. Now, stir in the hazelnuts. Now, knead the mixture to form a dough; place in the refrigerator for about 35 minutes. 3. To finish, shape the prepared dough into the bite-sized balls; arrange them on a baking dish; flatten the balls using the back of a spoon. 4. Mix granulated sweetener with ground cinnamon. Press your cookies in the cinnamon mixture until they are completely covered. 5. Bake the cookies for 20 minutes at 154°C. 6. Leave them to cool for about 10 minutes before transferring them to a wire rack. Bon appétit!

Simple Pineapple Sticks

Prep time: 5 minutes | Cook time: 10 minutes | Serves 4

½ fresh pineapple, cut into sticks	25 g desiccated coconut

1. Preheat the air fryer to 204°C. 2. Coat the pineapple sticks in the desiccated coconut and put each one in the air fryer basket. 3. Air fry for 10 minutes. 4. Serve immediately

Apple Hand Pies

Prep time: 15 minutes | Cook time: 25 minutes | Serves 8

2 apples, cored and diced	2 teaspoons cornflour
60 ml honey	1 teaspoon water
1 teaspoon ground cinnamon	1 sheet shortcrust pastry cut
1 teaspoon vanilla extract	into 4
⅛ teaspoon ground nutmeg	Cooking oil spray

1. Insert the crisper plate into the basket and the basket into the unit. Preheat the unit to 204°C. 2. In a metal bowl that fits into the basket, stir together the apples, honey, cinnamon, vanilla, and nutmeg. 3. In a small bowl, whisk the cornflour and water until the cornflour dissolves. 4. Once the unit is preheated, place the metal bowl with the apples into the basket. 5. cook for 2 minutes then stir the apples. Resume cooking for 2 minutes. 6. Remove the bowl and stir the cornflour mixture into the apples. Reinsert the metal bowl into the basket and resume cooking for about 30 seconds until the sauce thickens slightly. 7. When the cooking is complete, refrigerate the apples while you prepare the piecrust. 8. Cut each piecrust into 2 (4-inch) circles. You should have 8 circles of crust. 9. Lay the piecrusts on a work surface. Divide the apple filling among the piecrusts, mounding the mixture in the center of each round. 10. Fold each piecrust over so the top layer of crust is about an inch short of the bottom layer. (The edges should not meet.) Use the back of a fork to seal the edges. 11. Insert the crisper plate into the basket and the basket into the unit. Preheat the unit 204°C again. 12. Once the unit is preheated, spray the crisper plate with cooking oil, line the basket with baking paper, and spray it with cooking oil. Working in batches, place the hand pies into the basket in a single layer. 13. Cook the pies for 10 minutes. 14. When the cooking is complete, let the hand pies cool for 5 minutes before removing from the basket. 16. Repeat steps 12, 13, and 14 with the remaining pies.

Pumpkin Spice Pecans

Prep time: 5 minutes | Cook time: 6 minutes | Serves 4

125 g whole pecans	½ teaspoon ground cinnamon
50 g granulated sweetener	½ teaspoon pumpkin pie spice
1 large egg white	½ teaspoon vanilla extract

1. Toss all ingredients in a large bowl until pecans are coated. Place into the air fryer basket. 2. Adjust the temperature to 148°C and air fry for 6 minutes. 3. Toss two to three times during cooking. 4. Allow to cool completely. Store in an airtight container up to 3 days.

Ricotta Lemon Poppy Seed Cake

Prep time: 10 minutes | Cook time: 55 minutes | Serves 4

Unsalted butter, at room temperature	55 g coconut oil, melted
110 g almond flour	2 tablespoons poppy seeds
100 g granulated sugar	1 teaspoon baking powder
3 large eggs	1 teaspoon pure lemon extract
55 g heavy cream	Grated zest and juice of 1
60 g full-fat ricotta cheese	lemon, plus more zest for garnish

1. Generously butter a baking pan. Line the bottom of the pan with baking paper cut to fit. 2. In a large bowl, combine the almond flour, sugar, eggs, cream, ricotta, coconut oil, poppy seeds, baking powder, lemon extract, lemon zest, and lemon juice. Beat with a hand mixer on medium speed, until well blended and fluffy. 3. Pour the batter into the prepared pan. Cover the pan tightly with aluminum foil. Set the pan in the air fryer basket. Set the air fryer to 164°C and cook for 45 minutes. Remove the foil and cook for 10 to 15 minutes more, until a knife (do not use a toothpick) inserted into the center of the cake comes out clean. 4. Let the cake cool in the pan on a wire rack for 10 minutes. Remove the cake from pan and let it cool on the rack for 15 minutes before slicing. 5. Top with additional lemon zest, slice and serve.

Cream-Filled Sponge Cakes

Prep time: 10 minutes | Cook time: 10 minutes | Makes 4 cakes

Coconut, or avocado oil, for spraying
1 tube croissant dough

4 cream-filled sponge cake fingers
1 tablespoon icing sugar

1. Line the air fryer basket with baking paper, and spray lightly with oil. 2. Unroll the dough into a single flat layer and cut it into 4 equal pieces. 3. Place 1 sponge cake in the center of each piece of dough. Wrap the dough around the cake, pinching the ends to seal. 4. Place the wrapped cakes in the prepared basket, and spray lightly with oil. 5. Bake at 92°C for 5 minutes, flip, spray with oil, and cook for another 5 minutes, or until golden brown. 6. Dust with the icing sugar and serve.

New York Cheesecake

Prep time: 1 hour | Cook time: 37 minutes | Serves 8

170 g almond flour
85 g powdered sweetener
55 g unsalted butter, melted
565 g full-fat cream cheese
120 ml heavy cream

340 g granulated sweetener
3 eggs, at room temperature
1 tablespoon vanilla essence
1 teaspoon grated lemon zest

1. Coat the sides and bottom of a baking pan with a little flour. 2. In a mixing bowl, combine the almond flour and powdered sweetener. Add the melted butter and mix until your mixture looks like breadcrumbs. 3. Press the mixture into the bottom of the prepared pan to form an even layer. Bake at 164°C for 7 minutes until golden brown. Allow it to cool completely on a wire rack. 4. Meanwhile, in a mixer fitted with the paddle attachment, prepare the filling by mixing the soft cheese, heavy cream, and granulated sweetener; beat until creamy and fluffy. 5. Crack the eggs into the mixing bowl, one at a time; add the vanilla and lemon zest and continue to mix until fully combined. 6. Pour the prepared topping over the cooled crust and spread evenly. 7. Bake in the preheated air fryer at 164°C for 25 to 30 minutes; leave it in the air fryer to keep warm for another 30 minutes. 8. Cover your cheesecake with plastic wrap. Place in your refrigerator and allow it to cool at least 6 hours or overnight. Serve well chilled.

Cinnamon and Pecan Pie

Prep time: 10 minutes | Cook time: 25 minutes | Serves 4

1 pack shortcrust pastry
½ teaspoons cinnamon
¾ teaspoon vanilla extract
2 eggs
175 ml maple syrup

⅛ teaspoon nutmeg
3 tablespoons melted butter, divided
2 tablespoons sugar
65 g chopped pecans

1. Preheat the air fryer to 188°C. 2. In a small bowl, coat the pecans in 1 tablespoon of melted butter. 3. Transfer the pecans to the air fryer and air fry for about 10 minutes. 4. Put the pie dough in a greased pie pan, trim off the excess and add the pecans on top. 5. In a bowl, mix the rest of the ingredients. Pour this over the pecans. 6. Put the pan in the air fryer and bake for 25 minutes. 7. Serve immediately.

Gluten-Free Spice Cookies

Prep time: 10 minutes | Cook time: 12 minutes | Serves 4

4 tablespoons unsalted butter, at room temperature
2 tablespoons agave nectar
1 large egg
2 tablespoons water
240 g almond flour
100 g granulated sugar

2 teaspoons ground ginger
1 teaspoon ground cinnamon
½ teaspoon freshly grated nutmeg
1 teaspoon baking soda
¼ teaspoon kosher, or coarse sea salt

1. Line the bottom of the air fryer basket with baking paper cut to fit. 2. In a large bowl, using a hand mixer, beat together the butter, agave, egg, and water on medium speed until light and fluffy. 3. Add the almond flour, sugar, ginger, cinnamon, nutmeg, baking soda, and salt. Beat on low speed until well combined. 4. Roll the dough into 2-tablespoon balls and arrange them on the baking paper in the basket. (They don't really spread too much but try to leave a little room between them.) Set the air fryer to 164°C, and cook for 12 minutes, or until the tops of cookies are lightly browned. 5. Transfer to a wire rack and let cool completely. Store in an airtight container for up to a week.

Printed in Great Britain
by Amazon

16953520R00043